To my wonderful parents to whom I owe everything.
To Margherita and Valeria Simili – you have been a gift from
God into my life – I am forever in your debt.
To Andrew Russell, my soul mate, who never stopped believing in
the stories I had in my heart and who helped to make them shine.
To Luca and Antonella – my life.
To my students – the hope that the seeds of learning, the seeds
of knowledge that I have planted will continue to grow.

My hope is in teaching and giving…
Giving more, giving extra, giving everything.

Light of Lucia

A celebration of Italian life, love & food

La celebrazione dell'anima italiana

MURDOCH BOOKS

When I was a little girl I wanted to be a journalist and tell my stories to the world.

I had visions of owning my own restaurant. I desperately wanted to share with others the simple pleasures of good food, which my mum brought to our family table every day.

I also dreamt of travelling to many countries and have many stamps in my passport.

And travel I did.

In fact, it was while I was away from Italy that I identified more than ever with my Italian heritage. I learnt that my roots were real and true. All I had left to identify myself was my culture, which I embraced with all my heart. My very essence was already inherited: the intensity and the love of growing up in an Italian home. That made me, shaped me and sculpted me into the woman I am today.

These words of wisdom from my father have carried me through life: "Your culture is everything. If you lose that, you've lost all you ever had".

I did not open a restaurant, but instead opened a cooking school, Cucina Italiana, to teach my students how to recreate the time-honoured dishes my mother prepared for our family. Since then, I have shared with others my family's Italian cultural traditions – kept preciously intact for years. I never became a journalist either but here I am sitting down to tell you the story of so many lives.

I want this book to give the people I love something to hold onto and cherish forever. I aim to record and safeguard the Italian cooking heritage which has been lost in many misinterpreted recipes around the world.

I wish to bottle the tastes, the baking smells of my childhood. I aim to preserve the soul of Italian cooking – so rustic, so simple but so defined. As I wrote this book I reflected on how many people have touched and changed my life. I inherited knowledge and language from many countries, but no one was able to take away the Italian spirit deep in my heart.

Most of all, this book is an homage to many Italian immigrants around the world. This book has been designed to preserve the memories of the Italian families who have passed their culture to other countries, making our food one of the best in the world.

Wherever you may be, I want to provide you, the reader, with the knowledge to recreate Italian food. By reading this book you will learn to appreciate the best ingredients, how to intuitively judge a recipe and be confident in bringing many pleasures to your table.

A little girl called Lucia

As the chapters unfold, many tables are set, the scenery changes and you will be told the story of a little girl called Lucia.

We can see that little girl start to grow, listening attentively to stories told by the many generations of her family.

Lucia could be me, she could be you. She may be your neighbour, or any Italian woman around the world. I am telling you her story, using beautiful memories so you can identify yourself with this special girl.

Lucia is the light crying out not to be extinguished. Lucia's life is a reflection of this light which is inside every Italian life. It is the family, it is the Sunday lunches, it is our story.

Once upon a time, the story of Lucia began…

1

Battesimo

La nascita, la celebrazione del battesimo, parte della tradizione Cattolica.

The baptism
The birth, the celebration of baptism, the culture and Catholicism – all that is inherited from being born into the Italian way of life.

The first chapter of our lives is the birth and the christening, the start.

Once upon a time, there was a little seed growing inside a beautiful woman. That seed would grow and grow until one day that little seed came to life. For five generations my family has had many names carrying the *luce*, the light, and the hope that the Italian spirit would endure. *Light of Lucia* is the story of those generations. It is my story and my family's story. It is every woman's story and with it comes the hope that the *luce* will carry on. The seed of light represents not just another life; it represents the story of survival – for our culture, our art, our food and the life of our family.

"Lucia, oh Lucia! During life, there are many days you won't see the light. But the light is there inside of us. Feed your light. Keep it shining and keep the love of who you are strong and clear. If you keep it growing, your spirit will never die."

My father, Giuseppe Sampogna

The birth of a child.
I heard the sound of welcoming voices. I understood the tears, the smiles. I saw the glasses held high. I received colourful gifts, some made of gold, all of them representing love and birth and growth.

My life was about to start. Looking back, my father would always share memories of glory, nostalgic moments that brought tears to his eyes.

"Oh, this world," he would say. "It's so big and eccentric, yet so small."

The more we search in this big globe, the more we find our souls in small villages. We then discover we are small towns, not cities. We are communities searching for the same thing wherever we are.

I was baptised one month after my birth. And on that day, the Italian soul, *l'anima italiana*, with all its superstitions and traditions, glory and stories, would be carried out once again.

L'anima italiana is carried by every child born into an Italian family. Italians love life; we live for our family. We move hand in hand, expressing our feelings, and our days have a lot of colour, drama, exaggeration and comedy. With music in our ears, we can cry, love and make up in the same minute.

Our operas are loud; our art is simply *divina*. And we celebrate and celebrate.

To celebrate *il battesimo*, the baptism, we gather around tables and prepare typical dishes from our region. The newborn wears a beautiful white outfit, inspiring peace and purity. Blue or pink sugared almonds, *la bomboniera*, will be the gift you take home, along with precious memories you shared with the family. There's a new dress for *mamma* and a new suit for *papà*. The wine of the year is bought to remember the birth of your child and to honour the day. For us Italians, it is certainly one of the most important family gatherings of all.

This chapter will focus on antipasti recipes, which are an easy and successful way to mark a day of celebration like *il battesimo*.

125 ml (4 fl oz/½ cup) extra
virgin olive oil
1 garlic clove, finely chopped
3 handfuls black olives,
such as kalamata
A pinch of dried chilli
flakes, optional
1 handful oregano leaves
1 whole buffalo mozzarella, sliced

Sugo di pomodoro
2 tablespoons extra virgin olive oil
1 garlic clove, finely chopped
400 g (14 oz) tinned whole
tomatoes, puréed
Few basil leaves, torn

I first made this when friends came to visit unexpectedly. On that particular
day, I had plenty of lovely sugo di pomodoro left over from one of my cooking
classes. So I added some olives, served mozzarella on the side and there it was:
the perfect antipasto.

Ulive con Mozzarella

OLIVES WITH MOZZARELLA

To make sugo di pomodoro Place the oil and garlic in a frying pan over medium heat and cook
for 1 minute or until garlic is soft. Add the tomato and bring to the boil. Reduce heat to
low and simmer gently for 20 minutes. Add torn basil leaves, season with salt and pepper, remove
from heat and set aside. It makes about 375ml (13 fl oz/1½ cups).

Place oil and garlic in a separate frying pan over medium heat and cook for 1 minute or
until garlic is soft. Add sugo di pomodoro and simmer for 5 minutes.

Add olives and chilli flakes, if using. Check seasoning, remove from heat, place in a serving
bowl and scatter with oregano leaves and serve with sliced mozzarella on the side.

Serves 4

Light of Lucia Battesimo Baptism

2 tablespoons extra virgin olive oil
2 garlic cloves, finely chopped
18 large green prawns (shrimp),
peeled and deveined,
with tails left intact
1 small handful flat-leaf (Italian)
parsley leaves, finely chopped

Salsa
100 g (3½ oz) giardiniera (see
glossary) or other mixed pickles
1¼ tablespoons red wine vinegar
1 handful flat-leaf (Italian) parsley
1½ tablespoons salted capers,
rinsed (see glossary)
½ hard-boiled egg
1 anchovy fillet
200 ml (7 fl oz) extra virgin
olive oil

Simple and delicious, this recipe is perfect for entertaining. Pickles and anchovies give sharpness and bite to the salsa, which goes beautifully with the sweet prawns.

Gamberi Fritti

FRIED PRAWNS

To make salsa Place all ingredients except for the oil in a food processor and process until finely chopped. With the motor running, add the oil gradually. Season to taste with salt and pepper and add a little more vinegar, if necessary.

Place oil and garlic in a frying pan over medium heat and cook for 1 minute or until garlic is soft. Add the prawns and cook for about 1 minute on each side or until cooked through. Remove from heat, sprinkle with parsley and serve with the salsa on the side.

Serves 6

8 Japanese eggplants or 2 large
eggplants (aubergines)
Sea salt, for sprinkling
Extra virgin olive oil,
for shallow–frying
1 whole buffalo mozzarella,
cut into small cubes
Basil leaves, to serve

These involtini can also be done with thinly sliced zucchini (courgette). Roll, then secure with a toothpick. If you have left-over sugo di pomodoro (see p17), you can pour it over the involtini and bake them in a hot oven until golden and bubbling.

Involtini di Melanzane

EGGPLANT ROLLS

Wash the eggplants and remove the stem. Using a mandolin or very sharp knife, slice the eggplants lengthways into 5 mm (¼ in) thick slices and place in a colander. If using large eggplants, cut each slice in half. Sprinkle generously with sea salt and set aside for at least 30 minutes. Rinse eggplant slices thoroughly and pat dry with a cloth.

Heat some oil in a frying pan over medium heat and, when hot, add a third of the eggplant slices and cook for 2–3 minutes each side or until golden. You may need to reduce the heat so you don't overcook the eggplant. Drain eggplant on paper towels and season with salt and pepper. Repeat with remaining eggplant, adding more oil to the pan, if necessary.

Make little involtini by placing a cube of mozzarella on top of each eggplant slice. Roll slices into a cylinder and secure with a toothpick. Place on a serving dish and scatter with basil leaves.

Serves 6

Introducing the Simili sisters

Once upon a time in Bologna, two sisters, Margherita, known as Mita, and Valeria, or Vale Simili, owned a famous bakery. Every morning before adding any bread to their oven, the sisters would test the temperature first by cooking very thin sheets of bread dough, which they called *le streghe*, or 'witches', because they burnt easily. One particular day, they were very hungry and decided to eat *le streghe* but, like any self-respecting Italian, they first added a drizzle of extra virgin olive oil and a sprinkle of salt. Well, it was so wonderful and tasty they decided to make some more. This time they added the oil and salt to the dough before baking so it would become crunchier. *Le streghe* became a huge hit and was adopted by all of Bologna as its favourite snack. The recipe that follows is the original recipe, so embrace it, love it and be prepared for the highest praise when you make it.

500 g (1 lb 2 oz) plain (all-purpose)
flour, plus 20 g (¾ oz) extra
25 g (1 oz) fresh yeast dissolved in
250 ml (9 fl oz/1 cup) warm water
50 g (1¾ oz) lard
2 scant teaspoons sea salt
2 tablespoons vegetable oil
3 tablespoons extra virgin olive oil
Sea salt, for sprinkling
1 small handful rosemary
leaves, optional

Le Streghe delle Sorelle Simili

THE SIMILI SISTERS' 'WITCHES'

Place flour in a mound on a work bench and make a well in the centre. Pour in the combined water and yeast mixture and incorporate a little flour from inside the well into the mixture. Add the lard and combine with the yeast mixture, then continue incorporating the flour from inside the well until you have a custard-like consistency. Be careful not to break the well. Add salt into the well, incorporate the rest of the flour and begin to knead dough vigourously. If the mixture is sticky, add some of the extra flour. If dough is too firm or dry, sprinkle a little water on the bench and knead dough into it.

Once dough is soft but not sticky, knead and beat it by picking up the dough with your hands and throwing it back onto the work bench. Continue for 8–10 minutes or until smooth and elastic, cover with a bowl and rest for 45 minutes.

Preheat oven to 210°C (415°F/Gas 6–7). Take a handful of dough and roll out on a lightly floured surface until 1 cm (½ in) thick. Lightly dust with flour and fold in half. Put dough through pasta machine, starting on the widest setting and finishing when dough is about 2 mm (¹⁄₁₆ in) thick. Place the strips on an oven tray greased with vegetable oil, brush the top with extra virgin olive oil, then sprinkle with sea salt and rosemary if using. Using a pastry wheel cutter, roll over the strip of dough to perforate into pieces. Bake, turning the streghe once, for 10–12 minutes or until golden and crisp.

Serves 6

280 ml (10 fl oz) olive oil
3 red capsicums (peppers), cut into strips
4 firm eggplants (aubergines), cut into
cubes, sprinkled with sea salt for
30 minutes, rinsed and pitted
1 celery stick, sliced, leaves finely chopped
1 onion, thinly sliced
2 garlic cloves, finely chopped
1 teaspoon tomato paste
(concentrated purée)

175 g (6 oz/1 cup) green olives, pitted
40 g (1½ oz/¼ cup) salted
capers, rinsed (see glossary)
1 handful slivered almonds, toasted
50 g (1¾ oz) small raisins
2 teaspoons honey
125 ml (4 fl oz/½ cup) red wine vinegar
1 handful basil leaves, torn
6 mint leaves, chopped

Caponata is Sicily. It's *agrodolce*, sweet and sour. The name comes from *capone*, which refers to the Sicilian lampuga fish. Because the fish was expensive, many substituted it with eggplant. I call this version, with raisins and almonds, *caponatina*.

CAPONATA WITH RAISINS AND ALMONDS

Heat 3½ tablespoons of oil in a large frying pan over medium heat and, when hot, add the capsicum. Cook for a few minutes or until soft and skins have started to brown. Remove from heat, season and set aside.

Wipe pan with a paper towel, then add 3½ tablespoons oil. Place over medium heat and, when hot, add the eggplant. Cook, turning once, for 5 minutes or until cooked but still firm to the bite. Remove, season and set aside.

Wipe pan with a paper towel, then add 3½ tablespoons oil. Place over medium heat and, when hot, add celery and leaves and cook for 3–4 minutes or until just soft. Remove and set aside.

Wipe pan with a paper towel, then add remaining oil. Place over low heat, add onion and cook, stirring often, for 5 minutes. Add garlic and tomato paste and cook for 2 minutes. Return capsicum, eggplant and celery to the pan along with olives, capers, almonds, raisins, honey and vinegar and simmer for 10 minutes. If the mixture starts to get too dry, add a little water. Stir in basil and mint. Serve as an antipasto with fresh bread or as an accompaniment to a meat dish.

Serves 8 as a starter or 4 as a side dish

Light of Lucia Battesimo Baptism

3 red capsicums (peppers)
3 yellow capsicums (peppers)
2 large eggplants (aubergines), cut into cubes
2 large red onions, cut into wedges
6 large mushrooms, trimmed and cut into 8 pieces each
3 zucchini (courgette), sliced into 1.5 cm discs

3 garlic cloves, sliced
100 ml (3½ fl oz) extra virgin olive oil
500 g (1 lb 2 oz) couscous
40 g (1½ oz) unsalted butter
15 g (½ oz) tuma or ricotta salata (see glossary), crumbled
1 handful oregano leaves

Couscous is the Arab legacy to Sicily. The preparation of couscous symbolises happiness and abundance. Make sure you salt the water or cook the couscous in a homemade stock, which will elevate this dish into something special. Adding vegetables or meat will help it go a little further in feeding guests.

Couscous di Verdura

VEGETABLE COUSCOUS

Preheat oven to 200°C (400°F/Gas 6). Wash and dry capsicums, then place on a foil-lined oven tray. Bake for 30 minutes or until they have collapsed and skins have blackened. Remove from the oven, cover with foil and rest for 30 minutes before removing the skin and seeds. Tear into strips and set aside.

Meanwhile, sprinkle the eggplant with salt and place in a colander for 30 minutes. Rinse and pat dry.

Reduce oven temperature to 180°C (350°F/Gas 4). Place eggplant, onion, mushroom, zucchini and garlic on an oven tray. Drizzle vegetables with 80 ml (2½ fl oz/⅓ cup) oil, season and bake for 30 minutes or until all the vegetables are cooked. Check the vegetables frequently and remove any that are already cooked.

Meanwhile, prepare the couscous according to packet instructions. Place the couscous in a large frying pan over low heat and separate grains with a fork, gradually mixing in the butter and the remaining oil. Add all the vegetables to the couscous and mix well.

Place in a large serving dish, scatter with tuma and oregano leaves and serve.

Serves 6–8

12 mussels, scrubbed and bearded
12 scallops, on the half shell
with coral attached
12 oysters, freshly shucked
1 handful flat-leaf (Italian)
parsley leaves, finely chopped
3 garlic cloves, finely chopped

200 g (7 oz) dry breadcrumbs
1 small handful oregano leaves,
finely chopped,
plus extra to serve
1 tablespoon grated parmesan
extra virgin olive oil, for drizzling

This recipe combines parmesan with seafood, which is considered a sin by many Italians. But while in Bologna, I was lucky enough to have this gratin dish cooked for me by my friend, Pierino Jovene, a chef on the Amalfi Coast. I forgave him this sin because the dish was sensational. It makes a handsome addition to a buffet table.

Capesante, Cozze e Ostriche Gratinate

SCALLOPS, MUSSELS AND OYSTERS AU GRATIN

Place mussels in a large frying pan, add 250 ml (9 fl oz/1 cup) of cold water and cook over high heat just until shells open. Remove from pan and discard any unopened shells. Remove the top shells from the mussels, then divide all shellfish among foil-lined oven trays.

Preheat a grill (broiler) to high. Place the parsley, two-thirds of the garlic and breadcrumbs in a bowl and combine well. Place the oregano, parmesan and remaining garlic and breadcrumbs in another bowl and combine well.

Top the oysters and scallops with a teaspoon of the parsley mixture. Top the mussels with a teaspoon of the oregano mixture. Drizzle with oil and grill (broil) until the breadcrumbs are golden and crisp. Serve immediately, scattered with a little extra oregano.

Serves 4–6

Light of Lucia Battesimo Baptism

½ lemon, juiced
16 green prawns (shrimp),
peeled and deveined
2 tablespoons olive oil
1 garlic clove, bruised
1 handful finely chopped
flat-leaf (Italian) parsley leaves
300 g (10½ oz) green beans,
trimmed, cut into 1cm
(½ in) lengths

4 small carrots, peeled and
cut into 1 cm (½ in) cubes
500 g (1 lb 2 oz) zucchini
(courgettes), cut into 1 cm
(½ in) cubes
6 small kipfler (fingerling) potatoes,
peeled, cut into 1 cm (½ in) cubes
200 g (7 oz) cooked peas
375 ml (13 fl oz/1½ cups)
good-quality mayonnaise

My mum used to make this salad for special occasions. It was a great way of using up leftover vegetables and it is easy to prepare well in advance. While in Bologna, I was served this dish in a *cestino* or basket made of bread dough.

RUSSIAN SALAD

Pour lemon juice over prawns and set aside for a few minutes.

Place oil and garlic in a large frying pan over medium heat and, when hot, add the prawns and cook for about 2 minutes each side or until cooked through. Discard the garlic. Sprinkle the prawns with parsley and remove from heat. Cut 9 prawns into small pieces and leave the remaining whole. Set aside.

Cook beans in boiling salted water for 2 minutes or until cooked but still firm. Remove with a slotted spoon and set aside. Repeat with carrot and zucchini.

Place potato in a saucepan filled with cold salted water. Bring to the boil and cook for 5 minutes or until tender. Drain and set aside.

Put all vegetables in a bowl. Add mayonnaise and chopped prawns. Season to taste and mix well. Place salad in a serving bowl, top with remaining prawns and serve.

Serves 6–8

500 g (1 lb 2 oz) red
capsicums (peppers)
500 g (1 lb 2 oz) yellow
capsicums (peppers)
2½ tablespoons extra
virgin olive oil
2 garlic cloves, bruised

2 tablespoons salted capers,
rinsed (see glossary)
1 tablespoon chopped
oregano leaves
1 teaspoon dried chilli flakes
fresh bread, to serve

This is a classic dish for any occasion, whether served as an antipasto or as a side dish. This dish can be kept in the fridge for a few days. Do not substitute the red or yellow capsicums with green ones because they are not as sweet.

Peperoni alla Calabrese

CALABRESE-STYLE CAPSICUMS

Preheat oven to 200°C (400°F/Gas 6). Wash and dry capsicums, then place on a foil-lined oven tray. Bake for 30 minutes or until they have collapsed and skins have blackened. Remove from oven, cover with foil and rest for 30 minutes before removing the skin and seeds. Tear into strips and set aside.

Place the oil in a frying pan, add the garlic and cook over high heat for 1 minute. Add the capsicum strips and all the remaining ingredients, season to taste and cook for 2 minutes or until just warmed through. Serve with plenty of fresh bread.

Serves 6

Light of Lucia Battesimo Baptism

Crostini

Crostini were created in Italy as a way of using up old bread. My mother would cut stale bread into thin slices, brush it with olive oil and toast it in the oven. She then kept the crostini inside a sealed jar for our snacks and, let me say, they didn't take long to disappear. Nowadays, crostini are served at many celebrations. Crostini will keep in an airtight container for a few days, ready for a last-minute *aperitivo* if friends drop in.

Simply cut a French baguette into thin slices, brush with extra virgin olive oil and place on baking paper-lined oven trays. Bake at 200°C (400°F/Gas 6) until crisp, turning the slices so they are toasted on both sides. Be careful as they'll burn easily. Cool and store in an airtight container for a few days.

If you like, you can add 2 bruised garlic cloves to the oil and stand for 20 minutes or so, before brushing the bread.

Serve crostini with the topping of your choice or try the ones on the following pages.

Light of Lucia · Battesimo Baptism

2 large red or yellow
capsicums (peppers)
2 garlic cloves, bruised
100 ml (3½ fl oz) extra virgin olive oil
1 large eggplant (aubergine), cut
into 1 cm (½ in) thick slices
Crostini (see p35)
1 handful basil leaves

Let the vegetables provide some colour. The capsicums and eggplant will take you back to the magic of the Mediterranean. Remember that the green capsicums are bitter, so stick with the red and yellow options.

Crostini alla Campagnola

COUNTRY-STYLE CROSTINI

Preheat oven to 200°C (400°F/Gas 6). Wash and dry capsicums, then place on a foil-lined oven tray. Bake for 30 minutes or until they have collapsed and skins have blackened. Remove from oven, cover with foil and rest for 30 minutes before removing the skin and seeds. Tear into strips and set aside.

Place garlic in 3 tablespoons of oil and set aside.

Place remaining oil in a large frying pan over medium heat and, when hot, add eggplant in a single layer, season to taste and add a splash of water, being careful as the water will spit. Cover and cook for 5–6 minutes on each side or until golden. Remove from heat and set aside.

Remove garlic from oil, rub crostini with garlic, then top with capsicum and eggplant. Tear the basil leaves over the top, drizzle with some of the garlic oil and serve.

Serves 6

Light of Lucia Battesimo Baptism

60 g (2¼ oz) unsalted butter
60 ml (2 fl oz/¼ cup) extra
virgin olive oil
2 garlic cloves, bruised
1 small fresh red chilli, thinly
sliced, optional

500 g (1 lb 2 oz) mixed
mushrooms, trimmed
and chopped
1 handful flat-leaf (Italian)
parsley leaves,
finely chopped
Crostini (see p35)

You can use this mushroom topping in many other ways. It is wonderful served as a *contorno* (side dish), or as a sauce for polenta. It's important to keep in mind that the pan should be very hot when you add the mushrooms. Adding olive oil to the butter stops the butter from burning.

Crostini ai Funghi

CROSTINI WITH MUSHROOMS

Place butter, oil, garlic and chilli, if using, in a large frying pan over medium heat and cook for 1 minute or until garlic is soft. Add half the mushrooms. Stir vigorously so the garlic does not burn. Once most of the mushrooms have been nicely coated and start to reduce in size, push them to the side of the pan and add remaining mushrooms to the centre. This allows the uncooked mushrooms to cook in the hottest part of the pan and also to be coated by the juices already in the pan. Cook mushrooms for a few minutes or until most of the juices have evaporated. Add the parsley, season and remove from heat. Cool for a few minutes, then top crostini with mushroom mixture and serve.

Serves 6

Light of Lucia Battesimo Baptism

1 kg (2 lb 4 oz) pontiac or other
red-skinned potatoes
2 tablespoons flat-leaf (Italian)
parsley leaves, finely chopped
60 g (2¼ oz/⅔ cup) grated
parmesan
4 eggs

100 g (3½ oz) tuma (see glossary),
provolone or mozzarella, cut
into small cubes
100 g (3½ oz/1 cup) dry
breadcrumbs
Vegetable oil, for deep-frying

You'll find different combinations for croquettes all around the world. This
version combines potato with tuma – a Sicilian sheep's milk cheese. Or you
can substitute the cheese with leftover ragù.

Crocchette di Patate

POTATO CROQUETTES

Peel the potatoes, place in a saucepan of cold salted water and boil until tender. Drain well,
put through a potato ricer or masher, then return to pan over medium heat. Stir potato
for 2–3 minutes or until all moisture evaporates. Transfer to a bowl and add parsley and
parmesan. Make a well in the middle of the potato mixture and stir in 2 eggs, one at a time,
until the mixture is well combined. Season to taste. Shape the mixture into croquettes, about
2 cm x 5 cm (¾ in x 2 in), placing a cube of cheese in the centre of each.

Lightly beat the remaining eggs in a shallow bowl. Dip the croquettes into the egg, allow
excess to drain, then roll in breadcrumbs, pressing to coat well.

Heat oil in a deep-fryer or large, deep-sided saucepan until 165°C (320°F). Deep-fry
croquettes, in batches, for 3–4 minutes or until golden and crisp all over. If you are not using
a deep-fryer, you may need to reduce the heat a little so that the croquettes cook evenly.
Remove with a slotted spoon, drain on paper towels and serve immediately.

Serves 6

Light of Lucia Battesimo Baptism

285 g (10¼ oz/1¼ cups)
caster (superfine) sugar
30 mint leaves
8 ripe peaches
125ml (4 fl oz/½ cup) Cointreau
125ml (4 fl oz/½ cup) maraschino
(see glossary)

My memories of summer are laced with the unforgettable fragrance of peaches and mint. This dish is magic when served in the heat of a summer night and it tastes refreshingly good.

PEACHES WITH MINT

Place the sugar and mint in a teapot or heatproof bowl, pour in 750 ml (26 fl oz/3 cups) boiling water, stir to dissolve sugar and stand for 1 hour.

Meanwhile, drop the peaches into a large saucepan of boiling water for 5–6 seconds, remove with a slotted spoon, then refresh in iced water. Slip the skins off the peaches, then cut in half, remove the stones, slice into wedges and place in a bowl. Add the liqueurs, pour over the mint tea, cover and refrigerate for 2 hours. Half an hour before serving, remove peaches from refrigerator.

Serve peaches scattered with the torn mint leaves from the tea.

Serves 8

Pasta frolla

200 g (7 oz) unsalted butter,
chilled and chopped
300 g (10½ oz) plain (all-purpose)
flour, plus extra for dusting
2 large egg yolks
100 g (3½ oz) caster
(superfine) sugar

Walnut filling

5 eggs, separated
200 g (7 oz) caster (superfine) sugar
50 g (1¾ oz) unsalted butter, softened
30 g (1 oz) plain (all-purpose)
flour, sifted
Zest of 1 lemon
300 g (10½ oz) coarsely
chopped walnuts
Icing (confectioners') sugar, for dusting

This is an exquisitely nutty and excitingly different cake. *Frolla* means soft and crumbly, so while the pastry may break easily when you're lining the tin, once cooked it will melt in your mouth.

WALNUT TART

To make pasta frolla Place butter and flour in a food processor and process until mixture resembles coarse breadcrumbs. Add the yolks, sugar and 1 tablespoon cold water and process until the mixture just comes together. Form into a disc, wrap in plastic wrap and refrigerate for 30 minutes.

Preheat oven to 190°C (375°F/Gas 5). Roll out the pastry between 2 sheets baking paper until 7 mm (⅜ in) thick and use to line the base and sides of a lightly greased 24 cm (9½ in) springform cake tin. Trim the sides so it is 5 cm (2 in) deep (you will have some pastry left over). Prick the base all over with a fork and freeze for 15 minutes. Line pastry with baking paper, fill with dried beans or rice and bake for 15 minutes. Remove paper and beans and bake for 10 minutes or until pastry is dry. Reduce oven temperature to 180°C (350°F/Gas 4).

To make walnut filling Using electric beaters, whisk yolks and sugar for 10 minutes or until thick and pale. Beat in the butter, flour and lemon zest, then fold in the walnuts. In a separate bowl, whisk egg whites until soft peaks form, then fold into the mixture. Pour into tart shell, smooth top and bake for 20 minutes, turn the cake, cover with foil and bake for another 20 minutes or until a skewer inserted into the centre withdraws clean.

Remove from oven and cool in tin. Serve dusted with icing sugar.

Serves 10–12

Light of Lucia Battesimo Baptism

1 litre (35 fl oz/4 cups) milk
Zest of 2 lemons
6 eggs, separated
260 g (9¼ oz) caster (superfine) sugar, plus 3 tablespoons extra
120 g (4¼ oz) plain (all-purpose) flour, sifted

90 g (3¼ oz) dark chocolate, melted and cooled
1 sponge cake, about 500 g (1 lb 2 oz)
150 ml (5 fl oz) Alchermes (see glossary) or Cointreau mixed with a few drops of pink food colouring

Italians love sponge cake. We love it with custard or with layers of cream and consider it to be one of our most delicious desserts. Perhaps zuppa Inglese came about as a way of disguising old sponge cake that had become too dry to eat. In the south of Italy, they use meringue to cover the *zuppa*, as I have done here, while in Bologna they like to keep theirs rustically pink.

Zuppa Inglese

Place 900 ml (31 fl oz) milk and the lemon zest in a saucepan over high heat and bring to the boil. Remove from heat and stand for 10 minutes to infuse.

Using electric beaters, whisk the egg yolks and caster sugar for 5–6 minutes or until pale and thick and ribbons form when you lift the whisk. Add a pinch of salt and the flour and combine well. Stir in remaining cold milk, then add the warm milk and whisk until smooth. Transfer to a clean saucepan, whisk over medium–high heat and boil for 2 minutes, then reduce heat to low and whisk vigorously until custard is thick and smooth. Divide mixture among 2 bowls and stir the melted chocolate into one of the bowls. Cover the surface of the custards with plastic wrap and stand until cool.

Cut the sponge cake into 3 horizontal layers. Brush one layer with liqueur and place brushed-side down in the base of a heatproof serving dish, then brush top with liqueur. Top with cooled plain custard. Then repeat with another layer of sponge, liqueur and chocolate custard, finishing with remaining layer of sponge, brushed with liqueur on both sides. Cover and refrigerate for 2 hours. Preheat grill (broiler) to high, just before serving, whisk the egg whites with the extra sugar until stiff peaks form. Pile onto the trifle and cook under a hot grill until lightly browned. Serve immediately.

Serves 8

Light of Lucia Battesimo Baptism

2

Primi passi

Primi passi in cucina –
scoprire come nascono i
più importanti piatti della
cucina Italiana.

First steps
Discovering the basics and learning the most important steps in Italian
cooking: making pasta, gnocchi, risotto and polenta.

 In this chapter we cover the most important basics of Italian cooking. It is time for real growth – it is time to learn the basics of life – for us Italians it is almost like learning how to walk and talk and you certainly will need to know these recipes if you are using this book.

- Pasta fresca
- Gnocchi
- Polenta
- Risotto

"Here we go, Lucia. Now that you understand your balance, it is time to dance before you can really walk. Let's make fresh egg pasta, my dear." Nonna Lucia

The *secrets* of homemade pasta

"Lucia, here in Emilia, if you do not know how to make pasta when you turn eight you will not find a husband," my Nonna told me. Like many Italian girls, I was about five years old when I first learnt to balance different flavours, and to unlock the secrets of various pastas that are specific to each region. If I had grown up in Naples it would have been pizza, and so on for the different regions, each with their own speciality.

Nonna whispered the recipe in my ear: "Fresh pasta as they make it in Bologna has only two ingredients, my dear, eggs and flour." No salt as it will leave marks on the sheets of pasta. In Piedmont, they may add white wine to the dough; in Tuscany, they will add olive oil.

In Emilia Romagna, the birthplace of pasta, it was *pasta all'uovo* that I first began to master. I followed the instructions carefully and heard the words of wisdom from generations before me that often struggle to be heard in a fast-paced world.

"Listen," whispered my Nonna. "Listen to your heart. Breathe deep the weather and take in the challenge that lies ahead of you. Close your doors and windows and take the phone off the hook."

Nonna taught me to take my time. "Patience is required in kneading – caress the dough and do not use any type of strength. Listen to the symphony of God. The weather is talking and with this sound of music you will control the quantity of flour given to your dough."

Next Nonna taught me to dance with the dough, just by using the kneading movements of my hands, turning it around and around. I learnt to protect my dough, to give it warmth and to keep transferring the weight of my body, forwards and backwards, backwards and forwards. "The act of dancing is the act of kneading. You get one, you have the other," said Nonna.

"If you do not knead properly you cannot develop the gluten in the dough, which gives it elasticity, and therefore no matter how long you cook the pasta it will remain hard," my Nonna explained. "But if you over-work the dough, your pasta will be so soft that it will not be acceptable for anyone who knows about Italian taste and tradition."

Doing it properly, according to Nonna, is kneading the dough for about 6 to 10 minutes – in doing so, you have developed the gluten, which is the personality of the dough. This is the most important part of making pasta.

"As you create the gluten you create a 'man in a bad mood'," explains Nonna. "You got that man mad, you provoked him and he is angry at you. Don't panic. Let him rest for 30 minutes."

Nonna taught me that by letting your man rest and relax for 30 minutes he'll be able to forgive you. It's the same for gluten. If you try to work with dough that has not rested, you will work harder and harder and it will fight back every step of the way. All these procedures produce excellent pasta with the correct texture.

And, as Nonna explained, "Good pasta can take you many places. It can also make someone smile and steal hearts, too."

220 g (7¾ oz) type '0' flour
(see glossary)
2 eggs (about 60 g/2¼ oz each),
at room temperature

This recipe – the result of many years of cooking and learning – makes sublime pasta and is the starting point for all the other fresh pasta recipes in this book. So mark this page, you'll be referring to it again and again. As for pasta entirely by hand, for that you will need a patient Nonna and time for lots and lots of practise. The movements required are very hard to explain in words – please forgive me.

FRESH EGG PASTA

"And so how would you start, Lucia?" asks Nonna with a cheeky grin.

First, place the flour in a mound on a work bench and make a beautiful well in the flour. Now remember, start with 200 g (7 oz) of flour and keep an extra 20 g (¾ oz) aside to account for the unknown, the challenges the day will bring and, as Nonna reminds, "what God will have secretly prepared for you". Break the eggs into the well and, if you want coloured pasta (spinach for green, tomato purée for red) add those ingredients now.

Beat eggs with a fork like you would do for an omelette. Be sure to incorporate all the egg yolks with the whites; there should be no traces of yolks that haven't been properly beaten. Next, start slowly adding more and more flour from the inside walls of your well until the consistency in the centre is quite thick (but not too thick) and the liquid will not escape across the bench – it should have a custard-like consistency. Use a spatula and press the remaining flour from the well into the 'custard'. Keep on pressing the flour into the dough until all but the reserved 20 g (¾ oz) of flour has been incorporated. Cover the dough with a bowl and wash your hands. After drying your hands thoroughly, remove the bowl and check the consistency of the dough. Does it need more flour? You are checking to see if the dough is not so wet that it sticks to the bench; if it's too sticky, you will need to add a little of the reserved flour. But be careful as you do not want it to be too hard either.

Now, it's time for the magic to begin. It is time to create the gluten by dancing with the dough through the kneading process.

You should spend about 5–6 minutes kneading the dough, caressing it. And remember what my Nonna said, "If you know how to dance, you know how to knead". So keep transferring your weight onto the dough and start feeling the changes. There should be some elasticity there and the colour of the dough will have changed. After 6 minutes of kneading properly, your dough will be ready to rest. If, however, you are inexperienced in making dough, then knead for 10 minutes instead.

Now that the gluten is fully developed, you must let the dough rest. As I said earlier, men and gluten need about 30 minutes to calm down. Place the dough under a bowl to rest and relax during this sacred time. As the dough rests under the bowl it will drink the water from the atmosphere and its molecules will break and give it more resistance. It will also double in weight.

When the dough has rested, the gluten is calm and will finally let you work with it. Cut the dough into 2 equal parts. It is important to remember that while you work with one piece of dough, always make sure the remaining piece of dough is covered under a bowl so that it does not dry out. Do not use plastic wrap as it suffocates the dough. Slightly flatten one piece of dough with your hands and start putting it through the pasta machine, starting from the largest setting, number 1, and moving through the settings without skipping any numbers on the pasta machine until you reach number 6 or 7 (depending on your machine). You do not want the pasta 'sheets' too thick or too thin.

If making tagliatelle (see p59), place the pasta sheets on a tray sprinkled with flour and place in a well-ventilated spot or in front of a fan until the pasta is dry but still pliable. Pass the pasta sheets through the cutting attachment for tagliatelle on the pasta machine. Further dry the pasta on a clean broom handle suspended between two chairs. If you wish to store the tagliatelle for another day, you must leave it to dry thoroughly.

Serves 4

A tale about Tagliatelle Bolognese

In the year 1502, the great Lucrezia Borgia was preparing to marry her third husband, Alfonso d'Este, the Duke of Ferrara. This beautiful woman had amazing long blonde hair and attracted a great many suitors.

Lucrezia was not only known for her passion for the finer things in life and entertaining, but also for poisoning both her lovers and political enemies.

To mark the special occasion of the marriage, a Bolognese cook belonging to the noble Bentivoglio family was assigned the task of creating a pasta that brought to mind Lucrezia's long blonde hair. Thus was born tagliatelle. Since that day, tagliatelle has been the traditional pasta to be tossed with ragù Bolognese, explained Nonna.

"So why then did the spaghetti take the glory?" I asked Nonna. "Was the spaghetti Lucrezia's lover?" I asked. "Yes," said Nonna, "And maybe that is how the flavour of Lucrezia's poison tastes for all the people of Bologna."

You see, nothing insults the Bolognese more than when their typical dish – tagliatelle al ragù Bolognese – is called spaghetti Bolognese!

Light of Lucia Primi passi First steps

1½ quantities pasta fresca, cut into
tagliatelle (see p54)
Grated parmesan, to serve

Ragù Bolognese

45 g (1½ oz) unsalted butter, plus
extra to toss
3 tablespoons extra virgin olive oil
1 small onion, finely chopped
1 celery stick, including the leaves,
finely chopped
1 small carrot, finely chopped

50 g (1¾ oz) prosciutto or pancetta
(see glossary), finely chopped
1 chicken liver, veins removed, finely chopped
250 g (9 oz) minced (ground) beef,
not too lean
250 g (9 oz) minced (ground) pork
150 ml (5 fl oz) dry white wine
400 ml (14 fl oz) milk
Freshly grated nutmeg, to taste
400 ml (14 fl oz) brodo (see p84), heated
400 g (14 oz) tinned whole tomatoes, puréed

You can omit the liver, but give it a try. Milk is often omitted but it helps to
tenderise the meat and make the ragù creamier. That's how the Bolognese like it!

TAGLIATELLE BOLOGNESE

To make ragù Bolognese Place butter and oil in a large heavy-based saucepan over medium heat. Add onion and cook for 5 minutes or until translucent. Add celery and leaves and cook for a few minutes, then add carrot and cook for 2 minutes or until tender. Stir in prosciutto and, once heated through, add liver and cook for 1 minute. Add the meat slowly to the pan, breaking it up with a wooden spoon to prevent it from sticking, and cook until browned. Add wine and cook until evaporated or until most of the alcohol smell is gone. Add the milk and simmer for 10 minutes then season and add nutmeg to taste. Add brodo and puréed tomatoes and simmer over very low heat, stirring occasionally, for about 3 hours until thick and saucy.

Cook the tagliatelle in a large saucepan of salted boiling water until al dente. Transfer the tagliatelle in batches to a large serving bowl using a *mandolino* (see glossary) or slotted spoon, tossing in butter and ragù with each batch so that it is well combined and the tagliatelle does not stick. Serve topped with more ragù and a good grating of parmesan.

Serves 6

A tale about Lasagne

"Nonna. Nonna. La lasagne e Emiliana o Romana?" I asked.

When Nonna looked at me she saw her soul imprinted in my eyes. "Lucia, oh Lucia," said Nonna. "How curious you are… now who told you about the Romans? Was it the boy around the corner?"

"Si Nonna. Antonio told me the Romans created the pasta shape. He said they began adding vegetables in Marche, but in Emilia it became famous. Is Antonio telling me the truth?"

"Oh Lucia, you know the Roman boys with their charm and magic…" said Nonna. And so the story of lasagne begins.

Indeed, Antonio was right: this baked pasta dish originated in Roma. But then look what happened when it was discovered in the Marche region.

It is said *vincisgrassi* was created in 1799 by an Italian cook who wanted to impress Prince Windisch-Grätz, who was captain of the Austrian Army. *Vincisgrassi* is a form of lasagne that, as well as containing meat, includes ingredients such as mushrooms and prosciutto inside the ragù.

The recipe then travelled on to Emilia where the air of the pastures inspired cooks to use the region's parmesan; here the béchamel became a smooth, velvety sauce to complement the green lasagne sheets. You see in Emilia, the green represents everything fresh: green is for wellbeing; green is for spinach.

"And so Lucia, this is why you will find a different recipe for lasagne in each region of Italy," explained Nonna. "Most of us want to feed our family well and with all we have left in the fridge we created layers and layers, forming a dish that would be unique to us."

Light of Lucia Primi passi First steps

This dish originated in Rome but you'll find a different lasagne recipe in each region of Italy. Some add mushrooms, others eggplant or artichokes. In Emilia, they add spinach to the pasta – green representing freshness and wellbeing.

Lasagne Verdi alla Bolognese

SPINACH LASAGNE

To make lasagne sheets Follow the instructions on page 54 for making pasta fresca using the weights on the opposite page, placing chopped spinach in the middle of the flour well once the eggs have been beaten. Continue with the pasta instructions until you have made the dough. Set it aside to rest for 30 minutes. Divide the dough in 2 pieces and working with one piece at a time (covering the other with a bowl), put through the pasta machine starting at setting number 1 and working through the settings until you reach either number 6 or number 7 (this will depend on the pasta machine as to how thick the pasta is at setting 6). Cut the pasta sheets into 12 cm x 25 cm (4½ in x 10 in) rectangles, remembering to keep the cut sheets between 2 clean tea towels (dish towels) so that they don't dry out.

1 quantity ragù Bolognese
(see p59)
160 g (5¾ oz) parmesan,
finely grated
Lasagne sheets
3 large eggs
350 g (12 oz) type '0' flour
(see glossary)
100 g (3½ oz) cooked spinach

(about 250 g/9 oz raw), squeezed
in a tea towel to remove excess
moisture, finely hand-chopped
Béchamel
800 ml (28 fl oz) milk
80 g (2¾ oz) unsalted butter,
plus extra for greasing
80 g (2¾ oz) plain (all-purpose)
flour, sifted
Freshly grated nutmeg

Bring a saucepan of well salted water to the boil. Fill a large bowl with cold salted water. Cook the lasagne, in batches, in boiling salted water for 2 minutes, then refresh in cold water, place in a single layer on tea towel (dish towel)-lined trays and pat dry.

To make béchamel Place milk in a saucepan and bring to the boil, then remove from the heat. Set aside. In a separate pan, melt the butter over low–medium heat. Remove pan from the heat. Add the sifted flour to the butter in one go and whisk well. Return to the heat and whisk for 2 minutes. Remove the pan from the heat and add the hot milk at once, whisking until it reaches a nice, smooth consistency. Return to the heat and bring back to the boil. Remove from heat, season to taste with salt, pepper and nutmeg.

Preheat oven to 200°C (400°F/Gas 6). Butter a 25 cm x 15 cm x 4.5 cm (10 in x 6 in x 1¾ in) oven-proof baking dish and cover the base with a layer of pasta. Add one-third of the ragù and sprinkle with parmesan. Add another layer of pasta, half the béchamel and more parmesan. Repeat both layers, finishing with another layer of pasta, ragù and parmesan. Bake for 15–20 minutes or until golden and bubbling. Remove from the oven and stand for 5–10 minutes before serving.

Serves 6–8

The origin of Garganelli

"Once upon a time, many years ago," my Nonna explained, "A lonely housemaid was preparing dinner for the family in the town of Lugo, in Romagna. She made a beautiful *sfoglia* (pasta sheet), then started to prepare some tortelli. But when she finished making the tortelli, she realised she had a lot of fresh pasta left over.

"Italians have been through war and experienced many difficult times… so, for most Italians, throwing food away is totally unacceptable," Nonna continued. "The lonely housemaid sat at the table, feeling sad and worried, desperately trying to think of what to do with the leftover dough.

"Right next to the girl was a loom with piles and piles of clothes on it. The maid stared and stared at the loom and the clothes and suddenly, breaking into a big smile, she grabbed one of the long matches used to light the old fire stove. She then took a small piece of the leftover pasta and, using the matchstick, turned it around the loom, forming the now-famous garganelli."

Garganelli

200 g (7 oz) type '0' flour
(see glossary)
20 g (¾ oz) finely grated
Parmigiano-Reggiano,
plus extra to serve
2 eggs

Sausage ragù

20 g (¾ oz) unsalted butter
1 tablespoon extra virgin olive oil
1 onion, chopped
500 g (1 lb 2 oz) good-quality sausages,
skins removed, crumbled
150 ml (5 fl oz) dry white wine
200 ml (7 fl oz) hot milk
400 g (14 oz) tinned whole
tomatoes, puréed
50 ml (1¾ fl oz) meat stock

You need a special garganelli tray (see glossary) to make these, or, as the Italian cookery writer Marcella Hazan suggests, use a comb and a chopstick.

GARGANELLI WITH SAUSAGE RAGÙ

To make garganelli Follow the instructions on page 54 for making pasta fresca using the weights above, placing parmesan in the middle of the flour well, with the beaten eggs. When the pasta sheets are slightly dry but still pliable, cut into 3 cm (1¼ in) squares. Working with a few pieces at a time and leaving the others covered with a cloth, place a square of pasta on the diagonal in the middle of the garganelli tray, place a wooden stick on top and roll once to form a cylinder. Place on a tea towel (dish towel)-lined tray and repeat with remaining pasta.

To make sausage ragù Place butter and oil in a large saucepan over medium heat, add onion and cook for 5 minutes or until soft. Add sausage and cook until slightly dry and crisp. Add wine and cook until evaporated and the smell of alcohol is gone. Add milk and, once creamy, add tomatoes and stock, reduce heat to low and cook, stirring regularly, for about 1 hour or until thickened and reduced.

Cook the garganelli in salted boiling water until al dente, drain, reserving a little cooking water. Toss the garganelli with the ragù, adding 1–2 tablespoons of the cooking water to dilute the sauce, if necessary. Sprinkle with parmesan and serve.

Serves 4

Light of Lucia Primi passi First steps

Filling
500 g (1 lb 2 oz) ricotta
250 g (9 oz) grated parmesan,
plus extra for baking
1 handful chopped flat-leaf
(Italian) parsley
1 egg, beaten
Freshly grated nutmeg, to taste

Sauce
40 g (1½ oz) unsalted butter
2 x 400 g (14 oz) tinned
whole tomatoes, puréed
1 onion, quartered
125 ml (4 fl oz/½ cup) milk

Cannelloni
330 g (11¾ oz) plain flour
3 eggs
Unsalted butter, for greasing

Most Italians agree that the taste of the tomato sauce pinpoints where you're from in Italy. This dish is from Emilia Romagna, where locals often use butter to add a velvety texture, moisture and a touch of golden colour to their sauce.

RICOTTA CANNELLONI

To make filling Combine all ingredients in a bowl and refrigerate for 2 hours.

To make sauce Place the butter and tomatoes in a heavy-based saucepan over medium heat and bring to the boil. Add the onion and cook for 5 minutes. Add the milk, then reduce the heat to low and simmer gently for about 35 minutes. Do not worry if it coagulates – it will return to normal. There is no need to strain the sauce. Season and set aside.

To make cannelloni Follow the instructions on page 54 for making pasta fresca using the weights above. Cut pasta sheets into 10 rectangles, about 7.5 cm x 10 cm (3 in x 4 in). Remember to keep the cut sheets between 2 clean tea towels (dish towels) so that they don't dry out. Cook the pasta, in batches, in boiling salted water for 2 minutes, then refresh in cold water, place on tea towel-lined trays and pat dry.

Preheat the oven to 200°C (400°F/Gas 6). Spread 2 tablespoons of filling over each rectangle of pasta and roll up, starting at one long side, to form a cylinder. Place in a large, greased baking dish, seam side down. Cover with sauce, sprinkle with parmesan and bake for 15–20 minutes or until golden and bubbling. Rest for 5–10 minutes before serving.

Serves 4

Light of Lucia Primi passi First steps

It's time to make a decision: how much flour? Not too much and not too little. Do not worry. This gnocchi dish will be like learning to crawl. After all, it has eggs and parmesan, which will help it to bind, and you will not need to add so much flour. You can keep gnocchi for up to a day in the refrigerator, or they can be cooked, dried, then frozen. Once you are ready to use them, you can cook the gnocchi directly from the freezer.

POTATO GNOCCHI

Place potatoes in a saucepan of cold salted water and bring to the boil, then simmer until tender. Drain and, when cool enough to handle, peel and pass through a potato ricer or fine sieve directly onto a floured work surface. Add the butter and use a spatula to fold in. Because the potatoes will still be warm, the butter should mix in easily. Spread mixture out on a bench and let it cool down completely, this should take 15 minutes or so.

    Add the parmesan and keep using the spatula to amalgamate the mixture. Make a mound with the potato mixture. Open a well in the middle and add the egg. Beat the egg with a fork and start incorporating the potato mixture, slowly adding the flour until you have a soft but not sticky dough. Be careful you do not add too much flour too soon. Cover with a dry tea towel (dish towel) and stand for 30 minutes.

500 g (1 lb 2 oz) desiree potatoes,
unpeeled
20 g (¾ oz) unsalted butter,
softened
2 tablespoons grated parmesan,
plus extra to serve
1 egg
120 g (4¼ oz) plain (all-purpose)
flour (try to add less, if you can)

Now you need to test the dough to make sure it doesn't fall apart during cooking. To do this, break off a few small pieces and roll into a rough gnocchi shape, about 1 cm (½ in) in diameter. Then drop into boiling water to see if they hold their shape when cooked. If they collapse, you'll need to add a little more flour to the dough.

Roll out the dough on a lightly floured surface into long cylinders, about 1 cm (½ in) in diameter. Cut into 2 cm (¾ in) pieces and roll on the back of a fork to form ridges (this allows the gnocchi to hold the sauce). Place gnocchi on a tea towel that has been lightly floured.

To cook gnocchi, bring a large saucepan of well salted water to the boil over medium heat. Add gnocchi in batches and cook until they have risen to the surface. Leave them for a minute, then remove with a slotted spoon, place in serving bowl and toss with your favourite sauce (see recipes overleaf).

Serves 4

The pomodoro sauce is a classic one. Add the final touch of a few torn or whole fresh basil leaves. The gorgonzola sauce is deliciously rich. For children you can substitute the gorgonzola with the milder fontina cheese. The butter and sage sauce, however, is for the serious gnocchi eater who wants to appreciate each perfect gnoccho.

GNOCCHI THREE WAYS

Gnocchi al pomodoro Heat 1 quantity of sugo di pomodoro (see p17), toss through hot gnocchi with a handful of small basil leaves, sprinkle with parmesan and serve immediately.

Gnocchi al gorgonzola Place 180 ml (6 fl oz) milk and 20 g (¾ oz) unsalted butter in a small saucepan over medium heat and bring to the boil. Add 80 g (2¾ oz) of roughly chopped gorgonzola, fontina or gruyère cheese and stir until melted. Remove from heat and toss through hot gnocchi. Season to taste, sprinkle with grated parmesan and serve immediately.

Gnocchi con burro e salvia Place 150 g (5½ oz) unsalted butter and a handful of roughly chopped sage leaves in a frying pan over medium heat and cook until butter is just beginning to brown. Remove from heat, toss through hot gnocchi, season to taste, sprinkle with grated parmesan and serve immediately.

Perfect polenta

"Lucia, Lucia. You must learn to be patient. Stir and stir and learn the different tastes from all the northern regions," my Nonna told me. "Don't be in a hurry. Stand here with me and leave this busy world behind. Stand and stir and now add the polenta flour. See the colours change. See how beautiful the grains are as they break and become finer and finer. Master the consistency. Add the butter, the parmesan and let the world go by... take the time to remember the peace and warmth left by the generations before you who learnt to survive on this simple, peasant fare."

Christopher Columbus left the Americas for Italy in 1492 and he brought with him primitive grains that thrived in Italy's hot northern plains – particularly in Lombardy – where polenta has been a staple ever since. In fact, for centuries poor northern Italians survived on little more than polenta. In the south they even call the northerners polentoni (polenta heads).

Made and eaten straight away, polenta has a lovely soft texture that is perfect for rich saucy dishes such as stews and roasts, or calves' liver, in true Venetian style. If using polenta for grilling or baking, you'll need it to be *bella soda* (nice and firm). Pour it out on a wooden board and when set, cut with a wooden knife or string. Layer with fillings and bake it like a lasagne. Or it can be fried and served as an aperitivo or with fritto misto, chicken livers, salads or vegetables.

"Be careful you don't burn yourself," Nonna warned me, "As polenta spits like an angry woman when you are cooking it. And watch out if there are little children about because polenta will boil furiously and come down like the last days of Mt Vesuvius. Now Lucia, pay attention when stirring and see how your hand turns and turns..."

2 tablespoons olive oil
2 garlic cloves, finely chopped
400 g (14 oz) tinned whole
tomatoes, puréed
1.3 litres (45½ fl oz) vegetable
brodo (see p84) or water
250 g (9 oz/1⅔ cups) polenta

½ bunch cavolo nero (see glossary),
stems removed and finely shredded
200 g (7 oz) white cabbage,
shredded
25 g (1 oz) unsalted butter
50 g (1¾ oz) grated parmesan, plus
extra for serving

My son, Luca, won't eat this without a couple of fried eggs on top. The soft, runny yolks transform the flavours of this classical dish. Buy real polenta, the instant variety may save time but it won't deliver on flavour or texture.

Polenta con Cavolo Nero

POLENTA WITH TUSCAN CABBAGE

First prepare the tomato sauce by placing oil and garlic in a large frying pan over low–medium heat. Cook for 1 minute or until garlic is soft, then add tomatoes and simmer for about 25–30 minutes or until thickened and reduced. Season to taste.

Meanwhile, place stock or water in a large heavy-based saucepan and bring to the boil over medium heat. (If you are using water, add plenty of salt.) Add the polenta in a fine stream, whisking continuously to prevent lumps from forming. Continue stirring with a wooden spoon for about 2 minutes. Once it comes to the boil, reduce the heat to low and simmer until bubbles appear. Add the cavolo nero and cabbage and stir well. Continue to simmer, carefully as it will split, stirring occasionally, for about 40 minutes or until it pulls away from the sides of the pan. Then stir in the butter and parmesan.

To serve, spoon some tomato sauce on the base of a plate, then top with some polenta and finish with a little more tomato sauce. Serve immediately sprinkled with extra parmesan.

Serves 4

100 g (3½ oz) dried cannellini
beans, soaked overnight in
cold water
1 kg (2 lb 4 oz) tripe
1 lemon, halved
2 tablespoons extra virgin olive oil
1 garlic clove, finely chopped
1 onion, finely chopped

1 celery stick and leaves,
finely chopped
2 small carrots, finely chopped
2 tomatoes, chopped
3 bay leaves
1 teaspoon tomato paste
(concentrated purée)
1 litre (35 fl oz/4 cups) hot
vegetable brodo (see p84)

In Italy you learn as a child that you eat certain dishes on certain days of the week: "*Giovedì gnocchi, Venerdì pesce, Sabato trippa*" – Thursday's gnocchi, Friday's fish and Saturday's tripe.

MILANESE-STYLE TRIPE

Drain and rinse the beans, then place in a saucepan, cover well with cold water, bring to the boil, then simmer for 45 minutes or until tender. Drain the beans.

Wash tripe and remove all white skin, rubbing well under running water with lemon halves. Place tripe and lemon in a large saucepan, cover with cold water and simmer for 1 hour. Remove from heat, drain and, when cool enough to handle, cut the tripe into strips.

Place oil and garlic in a heavy-based saucepan over medium heat and cook for 1 minute or until garlic is soft. Add the onion and cook for 3–4 minutes or until translucent. Add celery and leaves and cook for 3 minutes or until soft, then add carrot and tomato and cook for 3 minutes. Add bay leaves and the tripe and cook for a few minutes or until heated through.

Add tomato paste and brodo, cover the pan and cook over very low heat for 1½ hours or until tripe is tender. If necessary, add a little extra water to prevent tripe drying out. Add beans, cook for 10 minutes, season and serve with plenty of bread.

Serves 6

Risotto *essentials*

"Now I will tell you how to make risotto properly," said Nonna. "My dear Lucia, you will need butter. The only exception will be when you make risotto with seafood. In that case, you would substitute the butter with olive oil and also add garlic. However, even then, I still add a touch of butter to the olive oil so that the rice will reach a higher temperature before adding the white wine. Then you must use parmesan of the highest quality, my dear – but of course not with seafood risotto cara Lucia. As for stock, it should be homemade as this is what really flavours the risotto. Never compromise on this. The rice will absorb all the liquid and triple in size and it will be flavoured with your wonderful stock."

In Italy there are three basic types of rice: arborio for a stickier risotto, such as Milanese-style with saffron; *vialone nano,* which produces a moister risotto, done *all'onda,* as the Venetians would, say. It suits their recipes well, as most of them are cooked with vegetables and seafood and deserve a little more liquid. Finally *carnaroli,* which, in my opinion, is the best of all as it's not too sticky or too wet. If this is your first time making risotto, *carnaroli* rice is probably the easiest rice to use as it has a perfect consistency. As always though, it is practice that will get you there. Cook with all three rices regularly and you will soon see the difference.

"Next, you need a good heavy saucepan, such as a cast-iron pot – a must if you like to cook risotto," my Nonna continued. "Concentration is key – keep an eye on that pot. And, finally, you must be patient – stir the risotto until it is ready, add the butter and the parmesan if it calls. Let it sit a little and off to the table you go."

2 large carrots, chopped
2 large onions, peeled
and quartered
2 celery stalks with the
leaves, chopped
500 g (1 lb 2 oz) beef soup bones
1 chicken carcass
1 piece of parmesan rind

Brodo is what every Italian needs in their kitchen. If there are three things we cannot live without, they are stock, parmesan and pasta. Make brodo in large quantities and freeze in small portions so you always have some on hand.

STOCK

Place all ingredients in a stockpot, add 8 litres (280 fl oz) of water, season well and simmer over medium heat for 2 hours. Strain the stock and enjoy the vegetables and meat as a light snack. Cool the stock, then refrigerate for up to 3 days or freeze in small quantities for up to 3 months.

To make vegetable stock, simply eliminate the meat.

To make chicken stock, use 2 chicken carcasses and eliminate the beef bones.

To make seafood stock, use a couple of handfuls of prawn shells instead of the meat. Taste the stock after 30 minutes of cooking and, if it's too strong, remove the shells and continue cooking.

Makes about 6 litres

3 red capsicums (peppers)
1.2 litres (44 fl oz) chicken stock
(see recipe opposite)
3 tablespoons extra virgin olive oil
60 g (2¼ oz) unsalted butter
1 onion, finely chopped

350 g (12 oz) carnaroli, arborio
or vialone nano rice
360 ml (12 fl oz) dry white wine
50 g (1¾ oz) parmesan, finely
grated, plus extra for serving
100 g (3½ oz) soft goat's cheese

This is one of the best risotto dishes I have ever created. The secret of a good risotto is to never let the rice go off the simmer.

Risotto con Peperoni

RISOTTO WITH CAPSICUMS

Preheat oven to 200°C (400°F/Gas 6). Place capsicums on a foil-lined oven tray and bake for 30 minutes or until skins have blackened. Remove and cover with foil. When cool enough to handle, peel, remove seeds and tear into strips.

Bring stock to the boil, then reduce to very low and keep simmering until ready to use (it's a good idea to also boil the kettle, in case you run out of stock).

Place oil in a large, heavy-based saucepan over medium heat, add 50 g (1¾ oz) of the butter and onion and cook for 3–4 minutes, or until translucent. Add rice and stir for 3–4 minutes, coating each grain with the oil. As the rice begins to absorb the oil and becomes translucent, add wine and stir until it has evaporated and the strong smell of alcohol is gone. Stir in the capsicums, then add a ladleful of hot stock and stir until it has been absorbed. Continue adding stock, one ladleful at a time. After about 18–20 minutes, the grains of rice should be plump and firm. It may need to cook for another few minutes. When ready, remove from the heat and stir in another ladleful of stock. (Don't worry: the rice is still cooking and you will need that extra bit of creaminess.) Stir in remaining butter, season to taste, then add the parmesan and goat's cheese. Let it stand for a minute or so. Then pour into a serving dish, sprinkle with a little more parmesan and serve immediately.

Serves 6

2 litres (70 fl oz/8 cups) milk
500 g (1 lb 2 oz) caster
(superfine) sugar
Zest of 1 lemon
150 g (5½ oz) arborio rice
Fresh fruit, to serve

This is the beginning of a famous recipe: Torta di Riso. As I started to make this cake one day, I found my children, Antonella and Luca, fighting for a spoonful of the creamy, sweet rice. Since that day, I only go as far as stage one of making the cake. During summer, when we have plenty of peaches, I add them to the dish.

ITALIAN RICE PUDDING

Place the milk, sugar and lemon zest in a large saucepan over low heat and stir until sugar dissolves, then increase the heat and bring to the boil. Be careful that the milk does not spill over. Once it comes to the boil, remove from heat immediately. Reduce the heat to very low, add the rice and stir with a wooden spoon. Cook uncovered, stirring often, for 2 hours. When ready, the mixture should be very creamy and the rice al dente. Serve immediately either on its own or with fresh fruit on the side.

Serves 8

3

Feste

La bambina cresce.
Ad ogni festa, un
piatto speciale.

Festivals
The little girl grows up in a world that is rich with superstitions and tales,
feast days and saints, celebrations and memories. To commemorate
each feast day, a special dish is created.

My childhood was one that unfolded like magic and my spirit has been imprinted with many lasting memories. I grew up on Catholic flavours, celebrating the Catholic festivals – amid the magical tales and surprises, the feasts with plenty of joy and lollies, saints and religion.

Remember *la Festa di Santa Lucia* on December 13? That was the saint who protected our eyes and brought lollies for the children. I recall leaving some grass on a plate and a bowl of water for her donkey because, oh yes, you will then get better presents and extra lollies, too!

I learned too that the period of *Natale* – the birth of Jesus – was for being at home with family and loved ones.

A few days later, during the feast of *San Silvestro* (on December 31) or *capodanno* (the first day of the year) there is always hope for new beginnings. This is when you get the opportunity to throw out the old and embrace the new… eat lentils and have prosperity, and wear red underwear for a better year.

Along with the everyday dramas and stories of growing up in a Catholic–Italian household, I learnt that my name – like many others – carries the name of a saint – a saint who would always protect me.

In Italy we have feast days for up to three saints every day of the year. So there's always a reason for another family reunion, another day to embrace as if it were a birthday, where we learn to give, to share, to love and to prepare big tables where we eat and drink in the name of God. And why not?

La Befana

January

S	M	T	W	T	F	S
1	2	3	4	5	6	7
8	9	10	11	12	13	14
15	16	17	18	19	20	21
22	23	24	25	26	27	28
29	30	31				

The real story of La Befana

Once upon a time in a small village lived an old woman called La Befana. One night La Befana heard a knock on her door. "Please open the door. Please help us." She opened the door to find three kings standing there, one of whom asked for directions.

"Do you know the way to Bethlehem?" he said.

"Aaah, it is not that easy to find," said La Befana. "You must go up and down the mountains and you must pass through many storms until you get there."

"Please, kind woman, take us to Bethlehem. We have an important mission. Today Our Saviour will be born," explained one of the men.

"I am sorry but I cannot come to Bethlehem with you," she answered.

"We all have missions," replied one of the men. "We all play a part in the world and we must help each other. Sometimes we have to spend days and nights crossing mountains and battling storms to reach closer to our dreams. To give someone a helping hand is to be a better person."

"I am not such a good person," came the reply. "Maybe one day I will change; maybe one day I will be able to help others. But not today."

La Befana closed the door and left the three men praying, asking for directions and guidance.

Suddenly a beautiful light invaded the whole village. It was the light that guided the three men to their destiny. This beautiful divine light also invaded the woman's little house.

"Go and search for the three men," said the light. "Look for hope. Look for another life. Be a good person and help others."

La Befana did not believe what she was seeing. How could a light be talking to her?

"I am your guardian angel," said the light. "Now go and shine your way to Bethlehem. Help the three men conclude their mission – they must be there for the birth of the baby Jesus."

La Befana moved quickly. She realised she had made a mistake and so off she flew on her broomstick. Although she spent many days and nights searching for the three men, she had no luck finding them.

When she finally returned home, she was sick and feeble. Before she died she prayed and prayed to Jesus. She prayed for forgiveness and begged for a day in the calendar year that she could help make a difference. Her dream was to visit children and bring them presents and lollies; she wanted another chance.

And now you see that is why La Befana exists on the Italian calendar. It's a day that we can all remember to be good and to make a difference in someone's life. Since then, every January 6 (which was the day the three men arrived in Bethlehem and gave baby Jesus many presents), this tale springs to life. On this day good children get the lollies and gifts, while the naughty ones receive a piece of coal. And of course there's the hope that all the little children will turn into good souls.

The menu which follows celebrates the end of our holidays. Parents go back to work and children go back to school.

45 g (1½ oz) unsalted butter
1½ tablespoons extra
virgin olive oil
3 garlic cloves, finely chopped
300 g (10½ oz) button mushrooms,
roughly chopped
300 g (10½ oz) field mushrooms,
stalks removed, roughly chopped

100 ml (3½ fl oz) dry marsala
300 ml (10½ fl oz) thickened
(whipping) cream
1 quantity pasta fresca, cut
into tagliatelle (see p54)
¼ cup coarsely chopped
flat-leaf (Italian) parsley
Freshly grated parmesan, to serve

To stop tagliatelle ribbons from sticking together, stir a little butter through the pasta before tossing with the sauce.

TAGLIATELLE WITH MUSHROOMS

Place 30 g (1 oz) butter, the olive oil and garlic in a frying pan over medium heat and cook for about 2 minutes or until soft. Add half the mushrooms and cook, stirring, until they are coated in pan juices and start to reduce in size. Push to the side of the pan and add remaining mushrooms to the middle of pan. This allows the uncooked mushrooms to cook in the hottest part of the pan and also be coated by the juices already in the pan.

Simmer, stirring occasionally, over low heat until most of the mushroom liquid has evaporated, then add the marsala and simmer until it has evaporated and when the strong smell of alcohol has disappeared. Add the cream and simmer gently for another 15 minutes or so to infuse the mushroom flavour.

Meanwhile, bring a large saucepan of water to the boil over medium heat. Add plenty of salt as soon as it reaches boiling point. A few minutes before the sauce is ready, cook the tagliatelle until al dente. Transfer the tagliatelle in batches to a large serving bowl using a *mandolino* (see glossary) or slotted spoon. Add some of the remaining butter and sauce to each batch, stirring continuously until all the tagliatelle has been added and is well combined with the sauce. Sprinkle with parsley and parmesan and serve immediately, with extra parmesan.

Serves 4

1 kg (2 lb 4 oz) whole snapper,
gutted and scaled
2 bulbs baby fennel, finely
chopped, fronds and
stalks reserved
3 garlic cloves, finely chopped
2 handfuls flat-leaf (Italian)
parsley, chopped
6 shallots, finely chopped

500 ml (17 fl oz/2 cups) white wine
125 ml (4 fl oz/½ cup) extra
virgin olive oil
1 tablespoon salted capers,
rinsed (see glossary)
40 g (1½ oz/⅓ cup) sultanas
90 g (3¼ oz/½ cup) green and
black olives
1 lemon, juiced

This is a truly special way to eat fish. The fennel, olives, capers and sultanas are almost a classic Sicilian approach.

Dentice con Finocchio

SNAPPER WITH FENNEL

Season the fish and place it in a shallow container. Finely chop the fennel fronds and stalks and combine with garlic, parsley, shallots and half the wine and half the oil. Pour over the fish, making sure it is well covered with the marinade, cover with plastic wrap and refrigerate for at least 30 minutes.

Meanwhile, prepare the stuffing. Bring a saucepan of salted water to the boil and blanch chopped fennel bulb for 1 minute. Drain and place in a bowl with the capers, sultanas and olives.

Half an hour before cooking the fish, remove it from the fridge and let it rest for 30 minutes at room temperature. Preheat oven to 180°C (350°F/Gas 4) and line a baking dish with foil. Remove the fish from the marinade, place in the baking dish, place the stuffing inside the cavity of the fish and pour over the marinade and the remaining oil. Bake for 20 minutes. Remove from the oven, pour over the remaining wine and the lemon juice, then cover with foil and bake for another 10 minutes or until fish is just cooked through.

Serves 2–4

250 g (9 oz) unsalted butter,
at room temperature,
or 250 g (9 oz) mascarpone
150 g (5½ oz) dark chocolate,
melted and cooled
2 tablespoons cooled espresso
25 cm (10 in) round sponge cake
80 ml (2½ fl oz/⅓ cup) Maraschino
(see glossary) or other cherry liqueur

80 ml (2½ fl oz/⅓ cup) Cointreau
80 ml (2½ fl oz/⅓ cup) brandy
Icing (confectioners') sugar,
for dusting

Zabaglione
7 egg yolks
150 g (5½ oz) caster (superfine) sugar
150 ml (5 fl oz) marsala

This lovely cake is from Liguria, which is located near the French border. Like their neighbours, the Ligurians have always loved cream and cake. This cake was created in 1875 by the Italian poet Giovanni Prati. He simply took a génoise (sponge) cake and added cream, then more cream. You need to start this cake the day before.

Torta Sacripantina

LIGURIAN CAKE

To make zabaglione Place egg yolks and sugar in a large heatproof bowl and beat with electric beaters for 5 minutes. Then add marsala and combine well. Place bowl over a saucepan of just-simmering water (make sure the base of the bowl does not touch the water) and whisk until mixture has doubled in size and holds a trail when the beaters are dragged through. Remove from heat and allow to cool completely.

Beat butter until creamy or, if using mascarpone, beat very quickly so it does not split and turn into butter. Add ¼ cup of the zabaglione to the butter or mascarpone and combine well. Add the remaining zabaglione, combine well and divide into 3 parts. To one part, add the chocolate, to another, the coffee, and leave the third plain.

Trim top and base from sponge and reserve trimmings. Cut sponge horizontally into three layers. In a bowl, combine the liqueurs and brandy and dilute with water so it will not be overpowering. Place a layer of sponge cake on a serving plate. Brush with the liqueur mixture and spoon over the coffee zabaglione. Repeat with another layer of cake, liqueur mixture and chocolate zabaglione. Top with the final layer of cake, brush with the liqueur mixture and cover the entire cake with the plain zabaglione. Refrigerate overnight.

Crumble over sponge trimmings and dust with icing sugar to serve.

Serves 8–10

Saint Valentine's Day

There are many myths of the origins of Saint Valentine's Day. One of them can be traced back to a priest called Valentino.

He lived in third-century Rome when it was ruled by Emperor Claudius II. The emperor was unhappy as the army was losing many wars and battles due to the lack of interest from soldiers who wanted to stay at home with their wives and families rather than go to war. So the emperor thought that if he forbade marriages, he would have a better chance of getting the soldiers off to war.

But Valentino had other plans. He began marrying young couples in secret. Eventually he was caught and imprisoned. Legend has it he received many flowers and gifts while in jail. He received particular interest from the daughter of one of the prison guards and, when he was beheaded on 14 February 269 AD, apparently his last message was a note to the girl saying "from your Valentine".

Today Saint Valentine's Day around the world is a day to say "I love you." But remember, it is a day for both of you. It's not a day for complicated recipes. Go out and make yourself beautiful. Stop to look at a new dress. Buy flowers and light candles and make your home feel special. And, if you are single, then please do not worry: you will fall in love and with the following menu – most of which can be done in advance – you cannot fail. Now take a big breath and relax – happy San Valentino.

250 g (9 oz) clams
250 g (9 oz) mussels
2 tablespoons extra virgin olive oil
2 garlic cloves, finely chopped
A very small pinch of
dried chilli flakes
200 g (7 oz) spaghetti or linguine
1 small handful chopped
flat-leaf (Italian) parsley leaves

Seafood is very simple to prepare and can be cooked in a few minutes while your pasta is boiling away. If you do not fancy seafood, then choose a pasta dish from another chapter. The secret is: don't stress. Nothing should be too difficult today.

La Spaghettata con Cozze e Vongole

SPAGHETTI WITH MUSSELS AND CLAMS

Wash and clean the shellfish, making sure you debeard the mussels. Discard any open shellfish. Place the clams in a bowl of cold water for 1 hour, changing the water at least four times, to remove the sand.

Place the oil, garlic and chilli in a large frying pan over medium heat. Once the garlic is soft, about 1 minute, add the shellfish, cover and cook for 3–5 minutes or just until shells open. Discard any that remain closed.

Bring a large saucepan of water to the boil over medium heat. Add plenty of salt, then add the spaghetti. Stir immediately to prevent the pasta from sticking.

Once pasta is al dente, drain and add to the shellfish with the parsley, toss to coat with sauce and serve immediately.

Serves 2

25 g (1 oz) unsalted butter,
at room temperature
75 ml (2½ fl oz) extra
virgin olive oil
1 small handful rosemary leaves,
chopped, plus 4 sprigs

1 small handful sage leaves,
finely chopped
2 teaspoons fennel seeds
3 garlic cloves, finely chopped
2 spatchcocks
150 ml (5 fl oz) thickened cream

This is a lovely dish served with roast potatoes or polenta. Make a wonderful sauce from the pan juices. Add the cream and deglaze the flavours in the roasting dish.

SPATCHCOCK WITH HERBS AND CREAM

Preheat oven to 200°C (400°F/Gas 6). Combine the butter, oil, herbs, fennel seeds and garlic in a bowl and season to taste. Rub mixture over each spatchcock and place some inside the cavity along with the rosemary sprigs.

Place the spatchcocks, breast side up, in a large flameproof roasting dish and bake for about 6–8 minutes or until golden. Remove from oven, turn them, baste with juices, reduce oven temperature to 180°C (350°F/Gas 4) and cook for another 10 minutes. Baste again, cover with foil and cook for another 15 minutes or until cooked through.

Remove from oven, place spatchcocks on serving platter and rest for 10 minutes. Meanwhile place ovenproof dish over a medium heat, add the cream and simmer, scraping up the bits from the base of the pan, for about 5 minutes or until cream has reduced and sauce has thickened. Place spatchcocks and any juices back in the pan for a few minutes to absorb the flavours, then serve.

Serves 2

Canola oil, for brushing
300 g (10½ oz/2 punnets)
raspberries, plus extra to serve
240 g (8½ oz) caster
(superfine) sugar
50 ml (1¾ fl oz) milk
4 eggs, separated
500 ml (17 fl oz/2 cups)
thickened (whipping) cream

This is a classic base for semifreddo. You can add any flavour you like; try strawberries or blackberries. This recipe makes enough for six, so if you're having a cosy dinner for two, you can always indulge in seconds or even thirds.

Semifreddo al Lampone

RASPBERRY SEMIFREDDO

Brush a 35 cm (14 in) terrine with oil, then line with plastic wrap.

Place 225 g (8 oz) of the raspberries in a saucepan with 2 tablespoons sugar and 80 ml (2½ fl oz/⅓ cup) of water and stir gently over medium heat for 2–3 minutes or until sugar dissolves. Remove from heat and cool.

Blend remaining raspberries with milk until smooth and set aside.

Place egg yolks and remaining sugar in a bowl and beat with an electric beater for 5–6 minutes, or until pale and creamy. Stir in raspberry milk and half of the cooked raspberries. Beat the egg whites and the cream in separate bowls until medium peaks form. Add the cream to the raspberry mixture, then fold in egg whites. Once well combined, pour into prepared mould and freeze overnight.

When you are ready to serve, remove the semifreddo from the freezer and leave for about 15 minutes in the fridge to soften. Top with remaining cooked raspberries and extra fresh raspberries and serve immediately.

Serves 6

Light of Lucia Feste Festivals

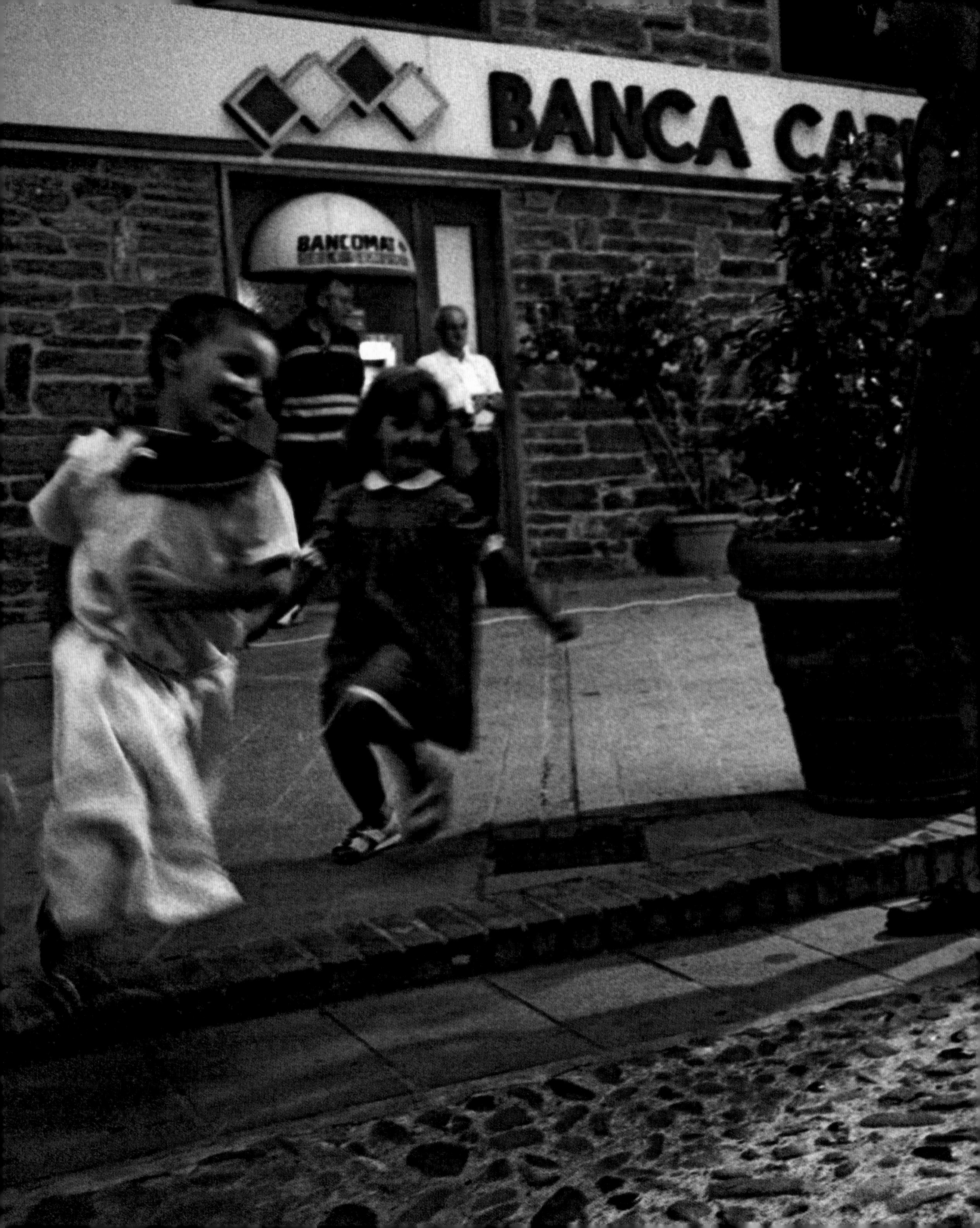
BANCA

Carnevale

February

S	M	T	W	T	F	S
1	2	3	4	5	6	7
8	9	10	11	12	13	14
15	16	17	18	19	20	21
22	23	24	25	26	27	28

Carnem levare in Latin means remove the *carne* – remove the meat from your menu. In Italy, Carnevale is a very important celebration, marking the beginning of Lent or *la Quaresima*. These days, from the north to the south, we wear masks, we dress up, we dance, we meet friends, and we celebrate. In the old days no meat, dancing or music was allowed during Lent, which marks the tragic events leading up to the death of Jesus.

The 40 days of Lent are followed by the celebration of Easter, one of the most important religious feast days of the year.

Today, rather than being seen as a time of strict abstinence, Lent is about dedicating time for reflection, respect and self-awareness and Carnevale remains a popular celebration. For the best Carnevale in Italy, you must visit Venice during February when wearing a mask is a must and the only good reason to remove it is to sample some of the city's best sweets.

3 large eggs
55 g (2 oz/¼ cup) caster
(superfine) sugar
Zest of 1 lemon
2 tablespoons extra virgin olive oil
60 ml (2 fl oz/¼ cup) rum
300 g (10½ oz) plain (all-purpose)
flour, sifted
Peanut oil or canola oil,
for deep-frying
Warm honey, to serve

These warm honey-drizzled pastries are typically found in Umbria during Carnevale.
They have almost a sweet bread flavour and are wonderful with a morning coffee.

Strufoli di Carnevale

FRIED CARNIVAL PASTRIES

Using an electric beater, beat the eggs and sugar for 8–10 minutes or until pale and fluffy. Add the lemon zest, olive oil and rum and mix well. Add the flour and mix until well combined.

Heat the oil in a large deep saucepan or deep-fryer to 165°C (315°F). Working in batches, use 2 spoons to shape the batter and and gently drop into the hot oil. The secret of deep-frying is to have a constant oil temperature. If you're not using a deep-fryer, you may need to turn the heat down to stop the oil from getting too hot or the pastries will brown too quickly. Deep-fry, turning to colour evenly, until crisp and golden, then drain on paper towels. Drizzle with warm honey and serve immediately.

Serves 6

Light of Lucia Feste Festivals

330 g (11¾ oz) ricotta
3 eggs
75 g (2½ oz/⅓ cup) caster
(superfine) sugar
45 ml (1½ fl oz) orange liqueur
1 teaspoon orange zest
150 g (5½ oz) plain (all-purpose)
flour, sifted
2 teaspoons baking powder
Peanut oil or canola oil, for deep-frying
Icing (confectioners') sugar, to dust

I make these in the morning, afternoon and even late at night. I absolutely cannot spend too many days without them. Nor can my kids.

Frittelle di Ricotta

RICOTTA FRITTERS

Place ricotta in a strainer over a bowl for at least 30 minutes to drain any excess water from the cheese. Put ricotta through a potato ricer or push through a fine sieve into a bowl. Place eggs and sugar in a separate bowl and beat with an electric beater for 3 minutes or until pale and fluffy. Add the liqueur and orange zest and beat for 2 minutes. Fold into the ricotta. Add the flour and the baking powder and mix until well combined.

Heat the oil in a large deep saucepan or deep-fryer to 165°C (315°F). Working in batches, use 2 spoons to form fritters and gently drop into the hot oil. The secret of deep-frying is to have a constant oil temperature. If you're not using a deep-fryer, you may need to turn the heat down to stop the oil from getting too hot. Fritters will expand upon cooking so don't overcrowd the pan. Deep-fry the fritters, turning to colour evenly, until crisp and golden, then drain on paper towels, sprinkle with plenty of icing sugar and serve immediately.

Serves 6

100 g (3½ oz) unsalted butter,
at room temperature
500 g (1 lb 2 oz) plain (all-purpose)
flour, plus extra for dusting
3 eggs
Zest and juice of 1 orange
50 g (1¾ oz) caster (superfine) sugar

45 ml (1½ fl oz) vin santo or sweet
liqueur (my Nonna uses grappa)
45 ml (1½ fl oz) milk
1 tablespoon olive oil
Canola oil, for deep-frying
Icing (confectioners') sugar,
for dusting

This sweet snack is found everywhere in Italy and it has a different name in each region – cenci, chiacchiere, bugie, sfrappole…

Crostoli

Place all the ingredients except the canola oil and icing sugar in a large bowl and stir until the dough comes together. Transfer to a lightly floured surface and knead dough for about 10 minutes or until nice and smooth. You may need to add a little more vin santo if dough is too dry. Wrap dough in plastic wrap and refrigerate for 1 hour.

Divide the dough in half. Working with one piece at a time and keeping the other half covered under a bowl, put one half of the dough through a pasta machine starting at setting number 1 through to setting number 6 until the dough is about 2 mm (1/16 in) thick. Using a crimped pastry cutter, cut the dough into rectangles, about 4 cm x 15 cm (1½ in x 6 in).

Heat the oil in a large deep saucepan or deep-fryer to 165°C (315°F). Deep-fry the crostoli in batches, turning to colour evenly, until crisp and golden. If you're not using a deep-fryer, you may need to turn the heat down to stop the oil from getting too hot or the crostoli may brown too quickly. Drain on paper towels, dust with icing sugar and serve.

Serves 6

March

S	M	T	W	T	F	S
1	2	3	4	5	6	7
8	9	10	11	12	13	14
15	16	17	18	19	20	21
22	23	24	25	26	27	28
29	30	31				

Festa della Donna

International Women's Day

In Italy we celebrate being a mother, a wife, a sister, a friend and a woman. Every woman, from mothers and mothers-in-law to young girls or old souls looking (or not) for love. *Festa della Donna* is considered to be one of the country's most beautiful celebrations. It is on this day that the country is carpeted in yellow, symbolic of mimosa or wattle.

If you go out to a restaurant you will be surprised to see a special menu dedicated to women, coloured and flavoured in yellow – from the vegetables through to the spices. I remember once on the streets of Firenze, many eyes turning towards me – a smile of acknowledgement, a smile of *tanti auguri signorina…* I will never forget that day.

1 litre (35 fl oz/4 cups) vegetable
brodo (see p84)
1 small onion, finely chopped
100 g (3½ oz) unsalted butter
500 g (1 lb 2 oz) Jap or butternut
pumpkin (squash), peeled, seeded
and chopped
350 g (12 oz) carnaroli, arborio
or vialone nano rice

185 ml (6 fl oz) dry
white wine
50 g (1¾ oz) parmesan, grated
plus extra for serving
¼ cup chopped flat-leaf (Italian)
parsley leaves

This is Veneto at its best. Make some fresh stock; it will help develop your
patience. That is all that is required for a good risotto. And do not forget
to add butter at the end. After all, you are in the north of Italy.

Risotto alla Zucca

RISOTTO WITH PUMPKIN

Bring the stock to the boil over medium heat, then reduce heat to low and simmer until
ready to use. (It's a good idea to put the kettle on in case you run out of stock.) Place the
onion and half the butter in a large, heavy-based saucepan over medium heat. Cook for
10 minutes or until the onion has become translucent, then add the pumpkin and cook,
stirring, for another 5 minutes.

Add the rice and stir well for 3–4 minutes to coat all the grains. Add the white wine and
stir until it has evaporated and the smell of alcohol has almost gone. Add a ladleful of hot
stock and stir until it has been absorbed. Continue adding stock, one ladleful at a time,
but only once the liquid has nearly absorbed. After about 18–20 minutes the grains of rice
should be plump and firm.

Taste to see if it is to your liking. It may need to cook for another few minutes. When ready,
remove from the heat and stir in another ladleful of stock. Stir in the remaining butter, season
to taste and add parmesan. Let stand for a minute or so. Pour into a serving dish. Sprinkle
with the parsley and a little more parmesan and serve.

Serves 4

Light of Lucia Feste Festivals

20 g (¾ oz) unsalted butter, plus
extra to toss through the pasta
1 garlic clove, finely chopped
100 g (3½ oz) picked cooked
crab meat
80 ml (2½ fl oz/⅓ cup) hot
vegetable brodo (see p84)

1 teaspoon saffron threads,
soaked in 30 ml (1 fl oz)
warm milk
50 ml (1¾ fl oz) thickened cream
1 handful flat-leaf (Italian) parsley,
finely chopped
300 g (10½ oz) fresh taglioglini

This easy-to-make dish is often found in the Veneto area. A love of saffron belongs to the Venetians and Lombards. Now it may belong to you.

Tagliolini al Granchio e Zafferano

TAGLIOLINI WITH CRAB AND SAFFRON

Place the butter and garlic in a frying pan and cook over medium heat for about 1 minute or until garlic is soft. Add crab meat and cook for 2 minutes. Then add 60 ml (2 fl oz/¼ cup) hot stock, saffron mixture and cream. Season to taste and simmer for 3 minutes. If it is a little dry, add more stock. Then add most of the parsley and turn off the heat.

Cook the tagliolini in plenty of boiling salted water until al dente. Transfer the tagliolini in batches to a large serving bowl using a *mandolino* (see glossary) or slotted spoon. Toss each batch with a little of the extra butter and sauce until the sauce is mixed through. Serve immediately with a little extra sauce and sprinkled with the remaining parsley.

Serves 4

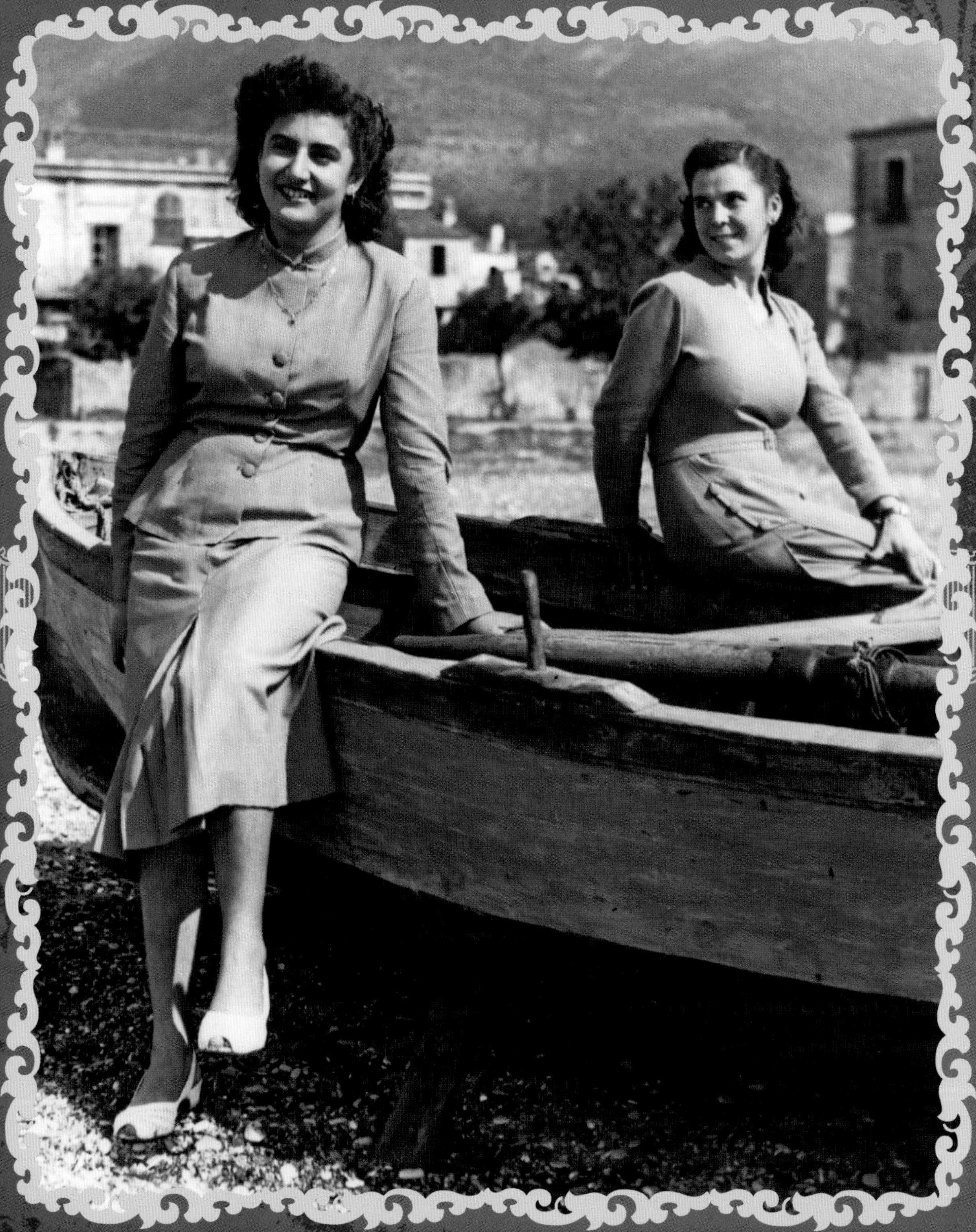

2 eggs, separated
50 g (1¾ oz) caster (superfine) sugar
100 g (3½ oz) mascarpone
60 ml (2 fl oz/¼ cup) limoncello
or Cointreau
Sliced fruit of your choice, to serve

This brings back memories of the Italy of old. Try it with fresh peaches, apricots or passionfruit.

Crema al Mascarpone

SWEET MASCARPONE CREAM

Using electric beaters, beat the yolks and sugar in a large bowl for 6–7 minutes or until pale and thick. Add the mascarpone and the liqueur and mix well, being careful not to over-beat the mascarpone or it turns into butter.

In a separate bowl whisk the egg whites with a pinch of salt until stiff peaks form, then very gently fold through mascarpone mixture.

Place some of the fruit of your choice in the base of serving glasses or bowls and top with the mascarpone cream. Refrigerate for 4 hours and serve topped with remaining fruit.

Serves 4

Festa di San Giuseppe

March

S	M	T	W	T	F	S
1	2	3	4	5	6	7
8	9	10	11	12	13	14
15	16	17	18	19	20	21
22	23	24	25	26	27	28
29	30	31				

Father's Day

For *La Festa di San Giuseppe*, we celebrate Jesus's father, Joseph or Giuseppe, and our own father, too.

Giuseppe is a name that is very symbolic for many Italians. It's a name that carries a lot of strength: San Giuseppe, the saint of the poor, the saint of the orphans, the one we pray to when we are in tough financial times. The table for San Giuseppe is full of promises: it is sometimes called *altare di San Giuseppe*, the altar of Saint Joseph.

Italians believe in a few elements that are sacred. They include: the water at the table, which represents grace and purity; wine, which is the benediction of God blessing us for all our work; and the lamp and the oil, which represent our faith.

Yes, we all have our problems, but San Giuseppe, our father, will protect us.

4 apples, peeled, cored and cut
into small cubes
125 ml (4 fl oz/½ cup) dry white wine
110 g (3¾ oz/½ cup) caster
(superfine) sugar
3 eggs
30 g (1 oz) unsalted butter,

350 g (12 oz) plain
(all-purpose) flour
60 ml (2 fl oz/¼ cup) Cointreau
at room temperature
Vegetable oil, for deep-frying
Icing (confectioners') sugar,
to serve

This particular recipe is from Ferrara and can also be served for *Carnevale*. It was once popular because it celebrated the use of lard. Of course, times have changed, so you will now be frying in vegetable oil.

APPLE FRITTERS

Place the apples, half of the wine and half the sugar in a bowl and set aside for a couple of hours to marinate.

Place the eggs, butter, flour, Cointreau, remaining sugar, remaining wine and a pinch of salt in the bowl of an electric mixer and beat for about 6 minutes or until a batter forms. Set aside for at least 30 minutes to rest.

Drain apples and add to the batter. Stir well to coat.

Heat the oil in a large deep saucepan or deep-fryer to 165°C (315°F). Working in batches, use 2 spoons to gently drop spoonfuls of batter into the hot oil. The secret of deep-frying is to have a constant oil temperature. If you're not using a deep-fryer, you may need to turn the heat down to stop the oil from getting too hot or the fritters will brown too quickly. Deep-fry the fritters, turning to colour evenly, until crisp and golden, then drain on paper towels. Dust with icing sugar and serve immediately.

Serves 6

500 g (1 lb 2 oz) pontiac
potatoes, peeled
3 eggs, lightly beaten
190 g (6¾ oz) caster (superfine) sugar
100 ml (3½ fl oz) extra virgin
olive oil
Zest of 2 lemons
15 g (½ oz) fresh yeast, dissolved
with a pinch of sugar in 125 ml
(4 fl oz/½ cup) warm milk

600 g (1 lb 5 oz) plain (all-
purpose) flour,
plus extra for dusting
Canola oil, for deep-frying
60 g (2¼ oz/½ cup) sifted icing
(confectioners') sugar combined
with 2 tablespoons
ground cinnamon
3 tablespoons warm clear honey

This recipe was my father Giuseppe's favourite. It carried his name. Some *zeppole* are made without the potatoes, but this one is light and you can feel the warm touch of the honey.

Zeppole di San Giuseppe

SAINT JOSEPH'S HONEY PUFFS

Place potatoes in a saucepan of cold salted water. Bring to the boil and simmer until tender. Drain and put through a potato ricer or push through a fine sieve into a large bowl.

Add the egg, sugar, olive oil, lemon zest and yeast mixture and mix well. Add the flour and mix until dough comes together. Turn out onto a floured surface and knead for 6 minutes or so. The dough should be soft but not sticky. You may need to add a little more flour or milk. Put the dough in a lightly oiled bowl, cover with a clean tea towel (dish towel) and leave to rest for 40 minutes to 1 hour or until doubled in size.

Heat the oil in a large deep saucepan or deep-fryer to 165°C (315°F). Working with one piece at a time, roll chestnut-sized pieces of dough into finger-length sausage shapes, cross the ends to form a loop and carefully drop into the hot oil. Cook until they rise to the surface, turn and cook until golden all over. Remove and drain on paper towels. Dust with combined icing sugar and cinnamon and pile on a serving platter. Drizzle with warm honey and serve immediately.

Serves 8

Light of Lucia Feste Festivals

April

S M T W T F S
1 2 3 4 5 6 7
8 9 10 11 12 13 14
15 16 17 18 19 20 21
22 23 24 25 26 27 28
29 30 31

Pasqua

Easter

Easter is about rebirth; it symbolises a second chance. In Europe, Easter also brings with it the arrival of spring and we celebrate the bounty of fresh fruits and vegetables delivered by the earth.

You will find eggs, vegetables and lamb being served all over Italy at this time of year. And the *Colomba Pasquale,* our traditional Easter cake baked in the shape of a dove, is here, there and everywhere.

Chocolate eggs are also in abundance, given as gifts to commemorate spring, fertility and new life. You can see the new life in the fields – there's rosemary asking to be picked to flavour that lamb that has been cooking for hours; there are changing colours of ripening fruits and blossoming flowers; and the noisy insects warning you there will be a warm summer ahead.

It is *Pasqua* and we celebrate once again with family.

50 g (1¾ oz) unsalted butter
1 tablespoon extra virgin olive oil
1 onion, finely chopped
500 g (1 lb 2 oz) English spinach,
leaves picked, washed, blanched,
squeezed dry and coarsely chopped

Freshly grated nutmeg, to taste
150 ml (5 fl oz) thickened cream
700 g (1 lb) ricotta
300 g (10½ oz) conchiglioni
(large shell-shaped pasta)
Freshly grated parmesan, to serve

This dish is so simple to make that you can enjoy it anytime. If your Easter is going to be about long lunches and feasting, then this dish or any of the other homemade pastas in this cookbook will be a huge success.

Conchiglioni con Ricotta e Spinaci

SHELL PASTA WITH RICOTTA AND SPINACH

Place the butter, oil and onion in a large frying pan over medium heat. Cook for 5 minutes or until the onion is soft, then add in the spinach and nutmeg. Stir in the cream and simmer for 2 minutes, then add the ricotta, season to taste and remove from the heat.

Meanwhile cook the pasta in plenty of boiling salted water until al dente. Drain, place in a large serving bowl, add the ricotta and spinach sauce and toss well. Serve immediately with sprinkled parmesan.

Serves 6

500 ml (17 fl oz/2 cups)
beef brodo (see p84) or water
80 ml (2½ fl oz/⅓ cup) extra
virgin olive oil
40 g (1½ oz) unsalted butter
1 kg (2 lb 4 oz) boneless lamb
shoulder, cut into large pieces

2 garlic cloves, finely chopped
2 sprigs rosemary
150 ml (5 fl oz) dry white wine
2 egg yolks, beaten and sieved
Zest and juice of 2 lemons

The secret to this recipe lies in the sauce which has lemon and egg yolks. In Italy, lamb is eaten at Easter to celebrate the arrival of spring.

Fricassea di Agnello

LAMB FRICASSÉE

Place the stock in a saucepan and bring to the boil, then simmer over low heat until ready to use.

Place half the oil and half the butter in a heavy-based casserole over medium heat. Sear the lamb until the pieces are nicely coloured on all sides. Place the lamb on a dish and set aside.

Remove the casserole from the heat and allow to cool completely. When cool, add the garlic and remaining oil and butter and cook over medium heat for about 1 minute or until garlic is soft. Be careful not to burn the garlic. Add the lamb and rosemary, stir for a few minutes, then add wine and simmer for about 15 minutes or until wine has evaporated and the alcohol smell has gone, then add the stock. Reduce heat to low, cover and cook for 1½ hours or until the meat is very tender. If necessary, add a little water so the lamb does not dry out.

Just before serving, combine the yolks, lemon zest and juice and stir into lamb until well combined. Cook over low heat for another 10 minutes until sauce has a creamy consistency. Do not allow to boil. Serve with vegetables of your choice.

Serves 6

300 g (10½ oz) plain (all-purpose) flour, plus extra for dusting
200 g (7 oz) chilled unsalted butter, chopped
2 yolks (from large eggs)
100 g (3½ oz) caster (superfine) sugar

Filling
400 g (14 oz) ricotta
400 g (14 oz) caster (superfine) sugar

1 tablespoon orange blossom water
3 tablespoons cedro (see glossary)
2 tablespoons finely chopped candied orange
400 g (14 oz) grano cotto per la pastiera (see glossary)
5 eggs, separated
Extra egg white, for brushing
Icing (confectioners') sugar, for dusting

Pierino Jovene was a charming chef and teacher from the Amalfi Coast. For Neapolitans, this cake is the symbol of Easter. Some say it was first made for Maria Teresa d'Austria, the queen who never smiled.

La Pastiera Napoletana

NEAPOLITAN CAKE

Place flour and butter in a food processor and process until mixture resembles breadcrumbs. Add egg yolks, sugar and 1 tablespoon cold water and process until mixture just comes together. Shape pastry into a ball, cover with plastic wrap and refrigerate for 30 minutes.

To make filling Place ricotta in a strainer over a bowl for at least 30 minutes to drain any excess water from the cheese. Combine ricotta with sugar, then stir in orange blossom water, cedro and candied orange. Add the grano cotto and egg yolks and combine well. In a separate bowl, whisk egg whites with a pinch of salt until stiff peaks form, then fold into ricotta mixture.

Preheat oven to 190°C (375°F/Gas 5). Roll out three-quarters of the pastry on a floured surface to 5 mm (¼ in) thick to line base and side of a greased 25 cm (10 in) springform cake tin. Trim any excess pastry. Spoon in filling, roll out remaining pastry, cut into strips and make a lattice over the top. Brush with egg white and bake for 30 minutes, then cover with foil, turn the cake around and bake for another 30 minutes. Serve dusted with icing sugar.

Serves 10

Light of Lucia Feste Festivals

La Festa della Mamma

May

S	M	T	W	T	F	S
1	2	3	4	5	6	7
8	9	10	11	12	13	14
15	16	17	18	19	20	21
22	23	24	25	26	27	28
29	30	31				

Mother's Day

If you are a mother, there is no better gift than the smile of your child and the smell of their body next to your skin. For mothers-to-be, enjoy this time – the birth and those first days of life that only you can sense; only you can feel. Bottle those memories; preserve them and keep them in your heart forever. Enjoy the growth and the waves of change.

To continue to develop is to be human – with new tastes, a new look, a new agenda and the latest cut and colour of jeans.

Mothers are always there – any time, any place – they are there for you. God bless all mothers for their splendid act of love – selfless, intense and infinite.

500 g (1 lb 2 oz) beef fillet, sliced
paper-thin
(ask your butcher to do this)
100 ml (3½ fl oz) extra virgin
olive oil
Juice of 1 lemon

2 young celery sticks, with the
leaves, finely chopped
1 handful flat-leaf (Italian) parsley,
finely chopped
Rocket (arugula) and shaved
parmesan, to serve

Sometimes you will see this wonderful dish with mushrooms, too. I prefer it just with celery and parsley. It is really refreshing.

Insalata di Carne Cruda alla Piemontese

PIEMONTESE-STYLE RAW BEEF SALAD

Place the beef slices in a shallow dish. Combine the olive oil and lemon juice in a bowl, mix in half the celery and parsley, then pour over the beef. Make sure the beef is well coated in the marinade. Season to taste, cover with plastic wrap and refrigerate for 30 minutes.

Place the beef and a little of the marinade on serving plates, scatter with the remaining celery and parsley and the shaved parmesan. Serve with rocket on the side.

Serves 4–6

80 ml (2½ fl oz/⅓ cup) extra
virgin olive oil
2 garlic cloves, bruised
1.5 kg (3 lb 5 oz)
cherry tomatoes
½–1 teaspoon dried chilli flakes
1 handful pitted black olives

400 g (14 oz) good-quality dried
spaghetti
1 handful flat-leaf (Italian) parsley,
finely chopped, plus extra
leaves to serve
Freshly grated parmesan, to serve

This is one of my favourite dishes. I love this dish because it is elegant and carries the best Italian flavours.

Pasta al Cartoccio

PASTA BAKED IN PAPER

Place the oil in a large frying pan over medium heat, add the garlic and cook for 2–3 minutes until garlic is soft and light golden. Add tomatoes and chilli flakes and cook for 5 minutes, then remove one-quarter of the tomatoes with a slotted spoon and set aside. Continue cooking, stirring occasionally, for 25 minutes or until sauce is thickened and reduced. Season and remove from heat.

Remove and discard garlic from tomato sauce, then place sauce in a food processor and process until smooth. Strain the sauce through a sieve and discard the skins. Return the sauce to the pan, add olives and simmer over a low heat until heated through.

Preheat oven to 200°C (400°F/Gas 6). Bring a large saucepan of water to the boil and add plenty of salt. Cook the pasta according to packet instructions but for only half the time specified. Drain well and toss with the sauce. Place 4 pieces of baking paper on a work surface and divide the pasta and reserved tomatoes among them. Sprinkle with the parsley, then fold the paper over to make 4 well-sealed parcels. Place on a large baking tray and bake for the remaining time suggested on the pasta packet or until al dente. Serve immediately, sprinkled with extra parsley and parmesan.

Serves 4

1 kg (2 lb 4 oz) Granny
Smith apples
3 eggs
120 g (4¼ oz) caster (superfine)
sugar, plus extra for sprinkling
Zest of 1 lemon
150 g (5½ oz) plain (all-purpose)
flour, sifted

165 ml (5¼ fl oz) milk
2 teaspoons baking powder
50 g (1¾ oz) unsalted butter,
chilled and chopped, plus extra
for greasing
Icing (confectioners') sugar,
for dusting

I've always loved this cake. It's great for afternoon tea or a late morning snack.
It really is home cooking at its best and easy enough that a child can make it.
And it's another precious recipe from Vali Simili (see p23).

APPLE CAKE

Preheat oven to 200°C (400°F/Gas 6). Peel, core, quarter and thinly slice the apples. Place the
eggs, sugar, lemon zest and a pinch of salt in a large bowl. Using electric beaters, beat until
thick and pale. Add the flour and milk and continue beating until well combined. Add the
baking powder, mix until combined, then add two-thirds of the apples.

Butter a round 25 cm (10 in) oven-proof dish and sprinkle the base with a little sugar.
Place cake mixture into dish, top with remaining apple, dot with butter and sprinkle with
sugar. Bake for 25 minutes, then cover with foil, turn cake around and bake for another
20 minutes or until a skewer withdraws clean. Serve warm or cold, dusted with icing sugar.

Serves 8

Light of Lucia. Feste Festivals

August

S	M	T	W	T	F	S
1	2	3	4	5	6	7
8	9	10	11	12	13	14
15	16	17	18	19	20	21
22	23	24	25	26	27	28
29	30	31				

Ferragosto

Summertime in Italy

On 15 August, Italians celebrate *Ferragosto*, which is one of our most important holidays. Today we celebrate the rise of Mary to heaven. But during the month of August we will also go on holidays. Yes, it's August and in Italy, it's hot!

It's time for blue skies, Vespa rides and a chorus of crickets. It's time for the best days of your summer holiday. It's about tanned bodies, short skirts and nail polish!

Let's watch the sun that never goes down. It's time for dining and laughing under stars and a guiding moon.

It's time for sitting under an olive tree, with the summer breeze, time to drive to fields of sunflowers or to the seaside.

It's a time for growing and sharing simple pleasures.

2 tablespoons extra virgin olive oil,
plus extra for drizzling
400 g (14 oz) tinned whole
tomatoes, puréed
1 handful basil leaves, torn
1.2 kg (2 lb 12 oz) eggplant
(aubergine), cut into 1 cm (½ in)
thick slices
200 g (7 oz) mozzarella, sliced
Freshly grated parmesan and fresh
herbs, for sprinkling

Pastry
300 g (10½ oz) unbleached
plain (all-purpose) flour
12 g (¼ oz) fresh yeast dissolved
in 130 ml (4½ fl oz) warm water
2 teaspoons salt

And so to the Simili sisters (see p23) once again. These two wonderful ladies taught me many exceptional lessons in every little corner of my life.

Torta di Melanzane

EGGPLANT PIE

To make pastry Place the flour in a mound on a work bench and make a well in the middle. Pour in yeast mixture and incorporate a little of the flour. Add the salt and incorporate the rest of the flour. Knead dough for 7–8 minutes or until it is springy to the touch. Cover with a bowl and rest for 40–50 minutes.

Meanwhile, place olive oil in a large saucepan over low heat. Add tomatoes and a pinch of salt. Cook for 20 minutes or until sauce has reduced and thickened. Remove from heat and stir in basil.

Heat a heavy-based chargrill pan over medium–high heat until very hot. Cook eggplant, in batches, on both sides until well browned and tender.

Preheat oven to 190°C (375°F/Gas 5). Roll out dough and line base and sides of an oiled 25 cm (10 in) springform cake tin. Place a layer of eggplant on the base, top with a layer of mozzarella, cover with one-third of the tomato sauce and season. Repeat twice more, finishing with a layer of tomato sauce. Drizzle with olive oil and sprinkle with parmesan. Bake for 45–50 minutes or until pastry is golden, turning it halfway through cooking. If it is browning too fast, cover with foil when you turn it. Rest for 30 minutes before serving (this makes it easier to cut into slices). Serve hot or at room temperature sprinkled with parmesan and fresh herbs.

Serves 6

Light of Lucia Feste Festivals

10 g (¼ oz) fresh yeast
500 g (1 lb 2 oz) type '00' flour,
plus 50 g (1¾ oz) extra
(see glossary)
90 g (3¼ oz/about 1) desiree
potato, peeled, cooked and mashed

1 tablespoon extra virgin olive oil,
plus extra for drizzling
1 small handful rosemary leaves,
coarsely chopped

The potato is the secret of this great focaccia. This is one of the best recipes
I have come across. Given that traditional focaccia recipes take a whole day
to make, this is relatively quick and simple and you are guaranteed success.

Focaccia Veloce

FAST FOCACCIA

Place the yeast and 250 ml (9 fl oz/1 cup) of warm water in the bowl of an electric mixer fitted
with a dough hook and stir to dissolve the yeast. Add some of the flour, then add the potato
and olive oil and keep mixing. Add 2 teaspoons salt and half the remaining flour and combine
on low speed, then add the remaining flour and continue to knead with the mixer for another
5 minutes. Place dough on a work surface and knead by hand for 3 minutes or until dough is
smooth and elastic. You may need to add a little of the extra flour if dough is sticky. Sprinkle
with flour, cover with a bowl and rest for 2 hours or until doubled in size.

Preheat oven to 210°C (415°F/Gas 6–7). Drizzle your hands with a little olive oil and place
the dough on a greased baking tray, about 30 cm x 45 cm (12 in x 18 in), stretching to fit.
With your fingers, make small indentations in the dough.

Sprinkle with sea salt and rosemary and drizzle generously with extra olive oil. Rest for
30 minutes, then bake for 15 minutes or until golden and crisp.

Serves 6

Light of Lucia Feste Festivals

November

S	M	T	W	T	F	S
1	2	3	4	5	6	7
8	9	10	11	12	13	14
15	16	17	18	19	20	21
22	23	24	25	26	27	28
29	30					

All Souls Day

The second day of November is the day we think of the loved ones that are no longer with us. For us in Italy, this is a day for remembering. We think of everyone who has died in different times, in different moments, in glory or despair. We think of how much we loved them and we often order a Mass on their behalf, particularly if they died in recent days.

We also pray for their souls and visit their grave. This is a solemn time for grieving and for silence.

300 g (10½ oz) dried broad
(fava) beans, soaked
overnight in cold water
125 ml (4 fl oz/½ cup) extra virgin
olive oil
1 small onion, chopped

1 ripe tomato, peeled,
seeded and chopped
500 ml (17 fl oz/2 cups) vegetable
brodo (see p84) or water
200 g (7 oz) wild fennel
(see glossary)
or fennel fronds, chopped

Maccu is a dish made with fava or broad beans. This classic Sicilian recipe is very simple and can be used in many ways. Try it as a first course, with some fresh crusty bread, then if there's any left over the next day, warm it up and toss through pasta. Wild fennel can be hard to find but fennel fronds are a good alternative. This recipe calls for a lot so you may have to ask your greengrocer to reserve some for you.

BROAD BEAN PURÉE

Drain broad beans and peel off outer shells.

Place 80 ml (2½ fl oz/⅓ cup) of olive oil in a saucepan over low heat. Add onion and cook for 5 minutes or until soft. Add tomato and stir for 2 minutes, then add beans, stock and the most tender parts of the wild fennel or fennel fronds, reserving some for serving. Cook, covered, for 1 hour, adding a little extra water, if necessary, until beans have turned into a purée. Season and drizzle with remaining oil. If you prefer a smoother texture, process in a food processor. Serve with crusty bread.

Serves 4

Note You can use the same quantity of fresh or frozen broad beans for this recipe. If using fresh broad beans, blanch podded beans briefly in boiling salted water, peel, then add as above but cook for only 25 minutes or until beans are very tender and breaking apart. Season to taste and purée until smooth, if you prefer.

December

S	M	T	W	T	F	S
1	2	3	4	5	6	7
8	9	10	11	12	13	14
15	16	17	18	19	20	21
22	23	24	25	26	27	28
29	30	31				

La Festa di Santa Lucia

Santa Lucia is the Saint of Light; the patron saint for little children and those who are blind.

The legend surrounding Santa Lucia – which dates back to the fifth century – is that she was so sad in heaven to see so many suffering children that she came to deliver presents and to give a little hope to such innocent souls.

This day was always my favourite day. It was a day I celebrated my name: Lucia. And a day my family celebrated the light.

On this day (particularly in Sicily) the tradition is to abstain from eating pasta and bread. Instead, they celebrate with dishes like cuccia and arancini filled with ragù or vegetables, with cream or lovely sweet flavours.

Enjoy this day. And if you have children, make it special for them.

400 g (14 oz) grano cotto per
la pastiera (see glossary)
60 g (2¼ oz) candied orange
90 g (3¼ oz) dark chocolate,
melted
Ground cinnamon, to sprinkle

Custard
500 ml (17 fl oz/2 cups) milk
Zest of 2 lemons
6 egg yolks
260 g (9¼ oz) caster
(superfine) sugar
60 g (2¼ oz) plain (all-purpose)
flour, sifted

For the day of Santa Lucia in Sicily, they prepare this sweet which is served inside a glass. This is a traditional dish and, in the old days, the recipe would vary depending on the budget of each family.

Cuccia di Santa Lucia

COOKED GRAIN CUSTARD

To make custard Place 450 ml (16 fl oz) of milk and lemon zest in a saucepan and bring to the boil. Remove from heat and stand for 10 minutes. Using electric beaters, whisk the yolks and sugar in a bowl for 5–10 minutes or until thick and pale. Add the flour and a pinch of salt and mix well. Add the remaining 50 ml (1½ fl oz) of milk, combine well, then gradually whisk in the warm milk mixture. Return to the pan and bring to the boil, whisking vigorously to prevent any lumps from forming. Reduce heat to low and cook the custard until thick and smooth.

Stir in the grano cotto, then add the candied orange and melted chocolate and combine well. Place in 6 individual serving glasses and serve sprinkled with cinnamon.

Serves 6

375 ml (13 fl oz/1½ cups) cold ragù
Bolognese (see p59)
60 g (2¼ oz) mozzarella, cut into
1 cm (½ in) cubes
155 g (5½ oz/1 cup) cooked peas
500 g (1 lb 2 oz) leftover cold risotto
2 large eggs

1 tablespoon finely chopped
flat-leaf (Italian) parsley
100 g (3½ oz/1 cup) dry
breadcrumbs
100 g (3½ oz) plain (all-purpose) flour
500 ml (17 fl oz/2 cups) vegetable
or peanut oil, for deep-frying

Once upon a time a bit of leftover ragù together with some leftover risotto was suddenly transformed into one of Italy's most-loved dishes. Remember many Italian dishes were created this way. Prepare the ragù a few days earlier and make plenty of it, then freeze it in small quantities ready for the day you feel like arancini or a nice plate of pasta.

Arancini

RISOTTO BALLS

In a large bowl, combine ragù with mozzarella and peas. With damp hands, mould risotto into balls about the size of a golf ball. Place a heaped teaspoon of ragù mixture into the centre of each ball and remould to seal filling.

In a shallow bowl, beat eggs, then season and stir in parsley. Place breadcrumbs in another shallow bowl and flour in a third bowl. Dust arancini in flour, then dip in egg mixture and finally coat with breadcrumbs, shaking off excess.

Heat oil in a large deep saucepan to 165°C (315°F). Fry arancini, in small batches, until golden brown all over. Drain on paper towels and serve immediately or, if necessary, place arancini on a baking tray and reheat for a few minutes in a preheated 180°C (350°F/Gas 4) oven.

Serves 6–8

Note Because no-one fries better than the Sicilians, here is a secret of theirs that I'll share with you. Make a *pastella* or batter by mixing 115 g (4 oz) of durum wheat flour with a little cold water to make a paste the consistency of pouring cream. Add a lightly beaten egg white and a little more water to make a thin batter. Then dip the arancini in the batter, coat in breadcrumbs and deep-fry as above.

Light of Lucia Feste Festivals

Vigilia di Natale e Natale

December

S	M	T	W	T	F	S
1	2	3	4	5	6	7
8	9	10	11	12	13	14
15	16	17	18	19	20	21
22	23	24	25	26	27	28
29	30	31				

Christmas

It is Christmas Eve, *La Vigilia di Natale*, in Italy and all the family will be reunited. This traditional family gathering is about more than opening presents, shopping centres and last-minute bargains. It is a sign of respect, of love for your family and love and acceptance of Jesus being born to save us. Most Italians do go to church at this time of the year. It is something that remains in our hearts. The day will also be busy with preparations for the special meal, which will take place on Christmas Eve.

The streets will soon be deserted as we gather inside our homes, counting our blessings and feeling the love that holds our families together.

There are many different ways in which Italians lead their lives. But there is something within us that holds us together and brings us back to the way we have been raised.

Perhaps it's a fear of the unknown. Maybe it's the mystic sense of divinity that makes us cling so close to each other. During an age where faith has lost its place, it's very reassuring to know that there is so much belief and hope and so many wishes upon stars.

On the night before Christmas – from the north to the south – all Catholics abstain from eating meat.

The menu will vary from region to region. In parts of southern Italy, for example, they have a traditional feast of seven fishes, perhaps representing the seven Catholic sacraments.

Christmas Eve is important to us all as it represents the final vigil before the birth of Jesus. After midnight Mass we exchange handshakes and kisses and wishes of *buon Natale*. *Babbo Natale* (Santa Claus) will then have to wait until after the midnight feast when the first presents will be exchanged. We then spend 25 December relaxing and eating leftovers from our Holy Night feast.

There might also be another church visit. More food anyone? It's not uncommon to find yourself in another relative's home enjoying another celebration. So in Italy, the menus for *La Vigilia di Natale* and *Natale* are very different and we never try and do both. We also start the preparations months in advance. On the menu you might find calamari, clams, *baccalá* (salted cod), artichokes, tortellini, capellacci, fennel, mandarins, *torrone* and chocolate. And for dessert, *panettone* and the lighter *pandoro* are popular throughout Italy.

1 large turbot, about 1 kg
(2 lb 4 oz), gutted
125 ml (4 fl oz/½ cup) good-
quality white wine vinegar
125 ml (4 fl oz/½ cup) dry
white wine
80 ml (2½ fl oz/⅓ cup) extra virgin
olive oil
2 garlic cloves, finely chopped
1 handful mint leaves

Turbot is a fairly large fish. If it's smaller, then adjust the cooking time accordingly. If you can't find turbot, other fish such as sole and John Dory will work equally as well. Choose a top-quality drop to complement the delicate flavour of the fish.

Rombo alla Mentuccia

TURBOT WITH MINT

Place the fish in a large ovenproof dish. In a bowl, combine the vinegar, white wine, olive oil, garlic and mint leaves. Pour over the fish, season, cover with plastic wrap and refrigerate for 1 hour.

Preheat oven to 210°C (415°F/Gas 6–7). Remove fish from the refrigerator 30 minutes before cooking and stand at room temperature. Bake for 10 minutes, then lower temperature to 180°C (350°F/Gas 4) and continue baking, basting fish with pan juices, for 20–25 minutes or until just cooked through. Serve immediately drizzled with the pan juices.

Serves 4

80 ml (2½ fl oz/⅓ cup) olive oil
1 tablespoon finely chopped onion
2 small green chillies,
seeded and finely chopped
1 tablespoon finely chopped garlic
16 large green prawns (shrimp) or
scampi, peeled and deveined
with tails left intact

100 ml (3½ fl oz) Cognac
2 quantities sugo di pomodoro
(see p17)
Few basil leaves, torn
1 handful flat-leaf (Italian) parsley,
finely chopped, plus extra to serve
400 g (14 oz) good-quality dried
spaghetti or linguine

Scampi is a variety of lobster. So during Christmas Eve, let the world go by while you enjoy your scampi and lick your fingers.

Spaghetti con scampi e Cognac

SPAGHETTI WITH SCAMPI AND COGNAC

Place the oil, onion and chilli in a large frying pan over medium heat and cook for 5 minutes or until the onion is translucent. Add the garlic and cook for 1 minute, then add the prawns and cook for another 3–4 minutes or until just cooked. Remove prawns from pan and set aside. Add Cognac to the pan and simmer until it has evaporated and the alcohol smell is gone, then add the sugo di pomodoro, basil and parsley and simmer for 20 minutes. Season to taste and remove from heat.

Meanwhile, cook the spaghetti in a saucepan of boiling salted water until al dente, then drain well. Return prawns to the pan, add drained pasta, toss with the sauce and serve topped with extra parsley.

Serves 4

80 ml (2½ fl oz/⅓ cup) extra virgin olive oil
2 garlic cloves, finely chopped
150 ml (5 fl oz) dry white wine
1 handful oregano, chopped, plus whole leaves, for garnish
1 large sole, about 1 kg (2 lb 4 oz), gutted and skinned on one side only (ask your fishmonger)

1 handful flat-leaf (Italian) parsley, finely chopped
30 g (1 oz) butter
30 g (1 oz) plain (all-purpose) flour
600 ml (21 fl oz) hot vegetable brodo (see p84)
1 large fennel bulb, thinly sliced and tossed with lemon juice and olive oil, to serve

This dish is elegant, easy-to-prepare and unique. The fish is done in a large frying pan and absorbs all the flavour of the herbs. A classic *vellutata* (velvety sauce) rounds out the dish.

Sogliola alla Saracena

SOLE SARACENA-STYLE

Place the olive oil and garlic in a non-stick frying pan large enough to hold the sole and cook over low heat for about 1 minute or until garlic is soft. Add wine and cook until nearly evaporated, about 5 minutes. Add oregano and the sole, skin side up. Season, add parsley and cover with a lid. Cook, without turning, for 15 minutes. Gently shake pan occasionally to prevent the fish from sticking.

Meanwhile, melt the butter in a saucepan over low heat. Stir in flour and cook for 2 minutes or until the mixture becomes sandy coloured. Whisk continuously, gradually adding in the hot stock. Simmer for 2–3 minutes, remove from heat and season.

When the fish is ready, pour sauce into the frying pan, shaking the pan so sauce covers entire fish. Garnish with oregano and serve immediately with the fennel salad.

Serves 4

4 sheets of rice paper
1 egg white
200 g (7 oz) honey
1 teaspoon vanilla essence
400 g (14 oz) icing (confectioners')
sugar, sifted
250 g (9 oz) blanched almonds,
toasted and chopped
250 g (9 oz) pistachios, toasted
and chopped

Torroncini make a beautiful present. Wrap them up in colourful paper, place inside a gift bag and give to your family and friends for Christmas.

LITTLE NOUGAT BARS

Line a 20 cm x 23 cm (8 in x 9 in) tray with 2 sheets of overlapping rice paper. Place egg white in a large bowl and using an electric beater, beat until firm peaks form. Add the honey and vanilla and beat until honey is incorporated. Gradually beat in icing sugar until thick and glossy, then transfer mixture into a heavy-based saucepan and stir over low heat for 10 minutes or until chewy.

Stir in nuts and remove from heat. Pour the mixture into prepared tin and spread evenly using a wet palette knife. Top with remaining rice paper. Let it cool, then cut into individual pieces. Store in an airtight container for 1 month.

Makes about 24 pieces

A festive tale about tortellini

"Let me tell you the story of tortellini," said Nonna. "There once was a beautiful *marchesina* visiting the town of Castelfranco Emilia. This little village was situated between two major cities: Bologna and Modena. The *marchesina* was tired of all her travelling, so she decided to spend the night in a small hotel. The hotel had a clever cook who had a treasured cookbook. But lately, the cook had felt sad. He lacked inspiration and found himself in a rut: instead of creating new recipes he had turned dusting the kitchen into an art-form. But the minute the cook cast his eyes towards the beautiful *marchesina*, he fell desperately in love.

"With his heart racing, he didn't waste a minute. She was the missing ingredient he needed to inspire new recipes. Wherever the *marchesina* went, the cook would follow, catching each breath, each movement, each step.

"Even when it was time for the *marchesina* to go to bed, he followed her. He wanted to catch the very last glimpse of her before nightfall. Through a very small keyhole he peeped and there it was. Her belly button.

"Racing to the kitchen he spent the whole night working on his new recipe. The following day as the *marchesina* came to dine she was met with the most beautiful bowl of pasta, shaped to look like her belly button and stuffed with a delicious mix of mortadella, prosciutto and pork. From that day on, tortellini became famous and a fixture on Christmas menus, especially in Bologna."

300 g (10½ oz) cold roast
pork, chopped
200 g (7 oz) mortadella, diced
150 g (5½ oz) sliced
prosciutto, diced
100 g (3½ oz) parmesan, grated,
plus extra for serving

1 egg, lightly beaten
A pinch of freshly grated nutmeg
4 litres (140 fl oz) beef brodo
(see p84)

Tortellini
550 g (1 lb 4 oz) type '0' flour
5 eggs

During Christmas time, you will see tortellini being sold everywhere in the streets of Bologna. It is more than tradition. It is a must. They will not compromise on the quality of their tortellini either. It has to be made fresh.

Light of Lucia Feste Festivals

Tortellini in Brodo

TORTELLINI IN BROTH

Place pork, mortadella and prosciutto in a food processor and process until finely chopped. Transfer to a bowl, add parmesan, egg and nutmeg, season and refrigerate until needed.

To make tortellini Follow the instructions on page 54 for making pasta fresca, using the above weights. Cut pasta sheets into 3 cm (1¼ in) squares. Place ½ teaspoon of filling onto each square, then fold diagonally, almost in half (a small triangle inside a bigger triangle) to cover the filling. Then bring the corners together, wrapping it around a finger to make the traditional tortellini shape. Place on a lightly floured tea towel (dish towel)-lined tray in front of a fan until dry.

Just before serving, place stock in a large saucepan over medium heat and bring to a simmer. Add tortellini and simmer until al dente. Serve immediately scattered with extra parmesan.

Serves 6–8

1 kg (2 lb 4 oz) Jap pumpkin
(squash), seeded and cut
into pieces
2 tablespoons extra virgin olive oil
150 g (5½ oz) grated parmesan,
plus extra to serve

1 egg, lightly beaten
Freshly grated nutmeg
2 quantities pasta fresca
(see p54)
1 quantity hot ragù Bolognese
(see p59), to serve

If my dear friend Renzo Franceschini, from Ferrara, is not in Italy at Christmas time, then he is certainly eating my *cappellacci di zucca*. For years I suggested bringing a new dish for our annual get-together but nothing else will tempt this wonderful man. He will make excuses and twist the story until he gets his beloved *cappellacci*. The flavour of the nutmeg comes alive in the filling, balanced by a beautiful ragù.

Cappellacci di Zucca

PASTA FILLED WITH PUMPKIN

Preheat oven to 200°C (400°F/Gas 6). Place the pumpkin on a baking tray, drizzle with olive oil, season and roast for 30 minutes or until tender. Once cooked, remove the skin, place the flesh in a large bowl and mash. Add the parmesan, egg and nutmeg to taste and set aside.

To make cappellacci Follow the instructions on page 54 for making pasta fresca. Cut pasta sheets into 7 cm (2¾ in) squares. Place 1 heaped teaspoon of filling onto each square, then fold diagonally in half and bring corners together to make a *cappellacci* shape. Place on a lightly floured tea towel (dish towel)-lined tray in front of a fan until dry.

Cook *cappellacci* in plenty of boiling salted water until al dente. Use a slotted spoon to scoop the cappellacci into a bowl and mix gently with the ragù. Serve with parmesan.

Serves 8

Light of Lucia Feste Festivals

30 g (1 oz) butter
2 tablespoons extra virgin olive oil
1.5 kg (3 lb 5 oz) piece chuck steak
1 large onion, finely chopped
2 celery sticks, finely chopped
1 carrot, finely chopped
400 ml (14 fl oz) Barolo, nebbiolo
or shiraz

400 g (14 oz) tinned whole
tomatoes, puréed
2 bay leaves
5 cloves
250 ml (9 fl oz/1 cup) beef brodo
(see p84)
soft polenta, to serve

This simple dish must be cooked and cooked and then cooked some more. Let the flavours blend, let the flavours develop. Time is everything. Only with time will the wine mellow so as not to overpower the dish. The cloves help accentuate the flavours. In Tuscany, while they may not use cloves, they do add Chianti and a little pancetta.

SLOW-COOKED BEEF

Place half the butter and half the olive oil in a heavy-based casserole over medium heat. When hot, add the meat and brown on all sides. Remove the meat and set aside.

Remove any fat from the pan, then add the remaining butter and oil and cook the onion for 3–4 minutes or until translucent. Add the celery and cook for 2–3 minutes or until soft, then add the carrot and cook for about 5 minutes. Return the meat to the pan, add the wine and stir well, scraping the base and side of the pan with a wooden spoon to remove any cooked pieces.

Next, add the tomato purée, bay leaves, cloves and stock. Season to taste and bring to the boil. Cover the pan and simmer gently over very low heat, turning often, for 3 hours or until the meat is very tender and starts to fall apart. Ensure the meat is always covered by the sauce. If it starts to dry out, add an extra ladleful of stock or water.

When the meat is cooked, remove from sauce, slice and place on a serving platter. Remove cloves from sauce, pour over the meat and serve with soft polenta.

Serves 6

December

S	M	T	W	T	F	S
1	2	3	4	5	6	7
8	9	10	11	12	13	14
15	16	17	18	19	20	21
22	23	24	25	26	27	28
29	30	31				

La fine dell'anno

New Year's Eve

Another year is coming to an end. Everyone is busy, from the north to the south of Italy. This is a day where we indulge many superstitious beliefs in the hope a better future will follow.

First of all, underwear must be bright red, which we believe will bring us good luck. Yes, we are a sexy nation and sexy red underwear is everywhere – ranging in style from the conservative to the eccentric.

If you are young – or young at heart – you may decide to go out for a dance after dinner.

The piazza is also the place to be for a last-minute, end-of-year gossip. As well as catching up with the latest fashion, you may meet your next-door neighbour's new lover, or discover who your cousin has his eye on. And be sure to keep an eye on the younger generation; their short dresses and hairstyles will make good conversation for the first month of the year.

In the South of Italy, cupboards are cleaned out. The old crockery will go. That chipped glass and broken vase are old news, out they go. It's a way to say "no" to the past and welcome the future.

Then it rings midnight. And with a shower of colours and fireworks the piazza comes to life. Cars and boats and bikes blow their horns, your glass of prosecco or spumante bubbles and everyone cheers.

Zest of 3 organic or
unwaxed lemons
500 ml (17 fl oz/2 cups) grappa
125 g (4½ oz) caster
(superfine)sugar

Limoncello is a refreshing and strong liqueur from the Amalfi Coast in the south of Italy. Enjoy this digestivo after your memorable New Year's Eve meal.

LEMON LIQUEUR

Place the lemon zest in a 1 litre (35 fl oz/4 cups) capacity sterilised bottle. Fill with grappa, seal and stand in a cool, dark place for 7 days.

Make a syrup by placing the sugar in a saucepan with 500 ml (17 fl oz/2 cups) of water over low heat, stirring until sugar dissolves. Bring to the boil, remove from heat and once cooled, pour into the bottle. Seal and stand in a cool, dark place for 30 days. When ready, strain mixture through a piece of muslin (cheesecloth) into another sterilised bottle and store in a cool, dark place or in the refrigerator for up to 6 months.

Makes 1 litre

1 cotechino, about 500 g
(1 lb 2 oz) (see glossary), soaked
overnight in cold water
2 bay leaves
300 g (10½ oz) Castelluccio lentils
(see glossary)
1 tablespoon olive oil

20 g (¾ oz) unsalted butter
1 small onion, chopped
1 young celery stick with leaves, finely
chopped separately
375 ml (13 fl oz/1½ cups) vegetable
brodo (see p84)

Eating pork today symbolises the richness of life. And, oh the lentils. No household in Italy goes without them at this time of the year. Like tiny little coins, the lentils represent numbers that you can count. But they are so plentiful that you will not be able to count them, suggesting prosperity, fortune and wealth for the New Year.

Lenticchie e Cotechino

PORK SAUSAGE WITH LENTILS

Drain cotechino and place in a large saucepan with bay leaves, cover with cold water and bring to the boil. Reduce heat to low and simmer gently for 2 hours. Drain.

Meanwhile wash the lentils in cold water and drain well.

Place the oil and butter in a large heavy-based casserole over medium heat, add the onion and cook for about 5 minutes or until translucent. Add the celery and celery leaves and cook for 3–4 minutes or until celery is lightly coloured. Add the lentils and enough stock to cover. Bring to the boil, reduce heat to low and simmer for about 40 minutes or until lentils are tender. Keep an eye on the saucepan as you may need to add extra stock if it dries out a little.

When you are ready to serve, slice the cotechino. If needed, gently warm the slices in a frying pan. Serve with the lentils.

Serves 4

4

Signorina

*La signorina studia
e si avvicina alla
cultura della tavola.*

Young lady
The little girl has grown into a beautiful young woman. She now studies
and loves to entertain friends. Although she has little time to spare from her
studies, she still cooks such classic, easy-to-prepare dishes as *pasta alla Norma*
and *penne alla vodka*.

Looking in the mirror I notice that my eyes seem rounder than ever. I'm wearing a delicate diamond cross necklace, a fine floral scent and a dress that traces my curves. With a brush of blush I colour my cheeks and comb my hair.

Looking down, I notice I'm still wearing my old *espadrilas*. I step out of them and into elegant high heels for the first time. It's in that moment that I leave behind that little girl and welcome a young woman. I step forward to embrace all that adult life has to offer. I remember seeing the world as shiny and inviting, full of colours and surprises and destinies that can unfold after a split-second decision.

Like many young women, I wanted to make the most of life, to discover in full the rules of love and the games that we play – games that make us smile; that make us cry. I put into practice all I knew – from the graceful movements I learnt in ballet, to the elegant style I copied from my older sister, to the words of wisdom taught to me by Mamma and Nonna Lucia; and the knowledge and faith delivered to me by my father.

"Remember, Lucia," said Nonna, "Sometimes we cry only to learn that laughing is coming right behind!"

When you are becoming a *signorina*, there are so many steps to go through. There are self-doubts and silly mistakes. But soon this will pass and a new time will come. You will start to entertain your friends and you will understand that all you have learnt at home is precious.

During this time of discovery, of friends and study and finding your feet, you will begin to fully appreciate the ease of good, quick pasta dishes like the ones my Nonna taught me.

Light of Lucia Signorina Young lady

80 ml (2½ fl oz/⅓ cup) extra
virgin olive oil,
plus extra for drizzling
2 garlic cloves, bruised
1 eggplant (aubergine)
1 handful basil leaves
400 g (14 oz) dried short pasta
such as farfalle or penne
Freshly grated parmesan, pecorino
or ricotta salata (see glossary),
to serve

Eggplant is a very important ingredient in Sicilian cooking and
they even use it as a base for their own pesto.

Pasta con Pesto di Melanzane

PASTA WITH ROAST EGGPLANT PESTO

Place the olive oil and garlic in a small bowl and, if time permits, cover and stand overnight to infuse. Remove garlic. Preheat oven to 200°C (400°F/Gas 6). Use a fork or skewer to prick the eggplant all over. Place on an oven tray, brush all over with some of the infused oil and roast, turning regularly, for about 30 minutes or until soft. Remove from oven and once cool enough to handle, remove the skin. Set aside to cool, then roughly chop.

Place basil leaves in a food processor with a pinch of salt and process for only a few seconds. Add roast eggplant and process gradually, pouring in the remaining infused oil until just smooth. Do not over-process. Season to taste, place in a bowl and drizzle with a little extra olive oil to prevent it from oxidising.

Cook the pasta in boiling salted water until al dente. Drain, reserving cooking water. Place pasta in a large serving bowl and add some pesto. For each tablespoon of pesto you use, add 2 tablespoons of the cooking water. Mix well and add a little more pesto and cooking water if necessary, so pasta is well coated in sauce. Serve immediately with parmesan.

Serves 4

Light of Lucia Signorina Young lady

1 kg (2 lb 4 oz) clams
80 ml (2½ fl oz/⅓ cup) extra virgin olive oil
2 tablespoons finely chopped shallots
4 zucchini, finely sliced
1 handful flat-leaf parsley, chopped, plus extra to serve

1 handful basil leaves, torn
1 garlic clove, finely chopped
125 ml (4 fl oz/½ cup) white wine
1½ quantities pasta fresca, cut into tagliatelle (see p54) or
400 g (14 oz) dried pasta, such as spaghettini

Lovely with fresh pasta such as tagliatelle but if time is short then a good-quality dried pasta will be equally impressive.

Tagliatelle alle Vongole

TAGLIATELLE WITH CLAMS

To remove the sand from the clams, place in a large bowl of water for a couple of hours, changing the water at least 4 times. Drain, then place in a large frying pan, add enough cold water to just cover the clams, cover pan and cook over high heat just until shells open. Drain clams, reserve the cooking liquid and strain through a tea towel (dish towel) to capture any unwanted sand. Discard any unopened shells.

Place 60 ml (2 fl oz/¼ cup) of olive oil in a large frying pan over medium heat, add the shallot and cook for 3 minutes or until translucent. Add zucchini and 250 ml (9 fl oz/1 cup) of the reserved clam cooking liquid and simmer for 5 minutes until the zucchini are al dente. Remove from heat, stir in parsley and basil, and season to taste.

Place remaining olive oil in a separate pan over low heat, add garlic and cook for 1 minute or until soft. Add clams and wine and cook, stirring, for a few minutes until the wine has evaporated and the smell of alcohol has almost gone, then add clams to zucchini sauce.

Meanwhile cook pasta in plenty of boiling salted water until al dente. With a slotted spoon or *mandolino* (see glossary), remove the pasta in stages and place in a serving bowl, tossing through some of the sauce to prevent the pasta sticking together. Serve topped with the remaining sauce, sprinkled with parsley.

Serves 4

140 ml (4¾ fl oz) extra
virgin olive oil
1 onion, finely chopped
200 g (7 oz) guanciale or pancetta
(see glossary), chopped
2 x 400 g (14 oz) tinned whole
tomatoes, puréed

1 small fresh red chilli (birdseye)
seeded and thinly sliced
450 g (1 lb) bucatini
Good-quality pecorino romano,
or parmesan, to serve

My father used to make this dish and I can never remember having a better *amatriciana* than his. For years I tried to learn his secret until finally I realised why his never tasted like any other: it was the *guanciale* (unsmoked Italian pork made from pig's cheek or jowls) he used to get from a friend. My father imprinted the aroma of this dish into our souls and with that he reassured us of his love for us.

Bucatini all' Amatriciana

183

BUCATINI WITH GUANCIALE AND TOMATO

Place olive oil and onion in a large frying pan over medium heat and cook for 3 minutes or until translucent. Add the guanciale and stir for a few minutes or until the fat becomes translucent. Add tomatoes and chilli, reduce heat to low and cook, stirring occasionally, for 20–30 minutes or until thickened. Remove from the heat and season to taste.

Cook the bucatini in a large saucepan of boiling salted water until al dente. Drain, and place in pan with sauce, return pan to medium heat and toss well to coat pasta in sauce. Place in a large serving bowl, sprinkle with pecorino romano and serve immediately.

Serves 4

Light of Lucia Signorina Young lady

80 ml (2½ fl oz/⅓ cup) extra
virgin olive oil
3 garlic cloves, finely chopped
½ teaspoon dried chilli flakes
2 x 400 g (14 oz) tinned whole
tomatoes, puréed
500 g (1 lb 2 oz) penne
2 tablespoons vodka
125 ml (4 fl oz/½ cup) thickened cream
1 handful flat-leaf (Italian) parsley,
finely chopped

This is a wonderful, easy-to-prepare dish, perfect for a late-evening meal
after a night out with friends.

Light of Lucia Signorina Young lady

PENNE WITH VODKA

Place the olive oil, garlic and chilli in a large frying pan over medium heat and cook for
1 minute until the garlic is soft. Add tomatoes and cook over low heat for 20–30 minutes
or until sauce has thickened. Remove from heat and season to taste

Cook the penne in boiling salted water until almost al dente. Drain and place in pan with
sauce, return to a medium heat and toss until pasta is well coated in sauce. Add vodka, mix
well, then pour in cream. Cover pan and and simmer for 1–2 minutes. Place in serving bowl,
sprinkle with parsley and serve immediately.

Serves 4

2 eggplants (aubergines)
Sea salt, for sprinkling
170 ml (5½ fl oz/⅔ cup) extra
virgin olive oil
2 garlic cloves, chopped
8 ripe tomatoes, peeled,
seeded and chopped,
or 400 g (14 oz) tinned whole
tomatoes, puréed

400 g (14 oz) spaghetti or
maccheroni
1 small handful basil leaves, torn
100 g (3½ oz) ricotta salata,
freshly grated
(see glossary)

This wonderful Sicilian dish pays homage to the Italian opera *Norma* by
Vincenzo Bellini.

PASTA WITH EGGPLANT AND RICOTTA SALATA

Cut the eggplants into small cubes and place in a colander. Sprinkle generously with sea salt and set aside for at least 30 minutes. Rinse eggplant thoroughly and dry with a tea towel (dish towel).

Place half the olive oil in a large frying pan over low heat, add the garlic and cook for 1 minute, or until garlic is soft. Add the tomatoes, increase heat to medium and cook for about 20 minutes or until sauce has thickened.

Meanwhile, place remaining olive oil in frying pan over medium heat and, when hot, add eggplant and fry until golden. Remove and drain on paper towel. Once tomato sauce has thickened, add half the eggplant to the sauce, season to taste and remove from heat.

Cook spaghetti in a large saucepan of boiling, salted water until al dente. Drain the pasta, reserving some of the cooking water. Place in a large serving bowl with sauce and mix well, adding a little of the cooking water to thin the sauce if necessary. Top with remaining eggplant, scatter with torn basil and serve immediately sprinkled with ricotta salata.

Serves 4

Light of Lucia Signorina Young lady

250 ml (9 fl oz/1 cup) extra
virgin olive oil
2 garlic cloves, finely chopped
2 small fresh red chillies, seeded
and finely chopped

1 handful chopped flat-leaf
(Italian) parsley, plus extra to serve
400 g (14 oz) spaghetti
Freshly grated pecorino romano
or parmesan, to serve

This dish breaks world records for being the fastest to prepare. It's the most famous pasta dish in our country. This pasta is perfect when you have an empty fridge and for those who simply do not want to cook. It's the easiest way to beat hunger and the dish that makes a regular appearance during the World Cup football final!

Spaghetti all' Aglio e Olio

SPAGHETTI WITH GARLIC AND OIL

Place all but 1 teaspoon olive oil in a saucepan over medium heat, add garlic and chilli and cook for 1 minute until garlic is soft, then remove from heat immediately. Quickly add parsley and reserved teaspoon of olive oil. That will stop the garlic from burning. Season to taste and set aside.

Meanwhile, cook spaghetti in plenty of boiling salted water until al dente. Drain and place in a large serving bowl with garlic oil and toss well. Sprinkle with extra parsley and serve with plenty of pecorino romano or parmesan.

Serves 4

Light of Lucia Signorina Young lady

750 g (1 lb 10 oz) strawberries
(about 3 punnets)
460 g (1 lb) caster (superfine) sugar
350 ml (12 fl oz) sweet vermouth
such as Martini Bianco
Mint leaves, to serve
Ice-cream, to serve, optional

This family recipe was measured in the typical Italian fashion: sometimes a little bit more sugar, sometimes a little bit more alcohol. When I want to add some charm to a homemade cake, these strawberries are served on the side, adding colour and a kick that only vermouth can deliver. You need to start this recipe the day before.

Fragole al Martini

MARTINI STRAWBERRIES

Hull strawberries and slice into a bowl. Add sugar and vermouth and refrigerate overnight. Half an hour before serving, remove from refrigerator. When ready to serve, tear mint leaves over the strawberries and serve with ice-cream or on their own.

Serves 6

Light of Lucia Signorina Young lady

5

Innamorata

E finalmente eccolo l'amore! Il più affascinante gesto di autoscoperta.

Falling in love
The beautiful Lucia finds love and she woos her bello with heart-warming soups, homemade pizza and finally captures his heart forever with some deliciously decadent desserts.

And off I went to discover the world. On a Vespa, I crossed the town and then travelled the world. Although I conquered hearts, I had not found my one special love. On and on I travelled.

Finally, in the crowd, one face clearly stood out. In one of the small aperitivi bars, one hot summer night I met the man of my life.

It's time to conquer. It's time to disguise the feelings that should not yet be revealed. Love is, after all, a game and one you must survive. Survive the nights he will not call, or the days he will arrive late.Yes, I fell in love. It happened to me as it happens to us all. I stayed up late. I learnt that the baker opens his doors for his loved ones, the lonely ones, the hungry ones.

Falling in love is one of life's most beautiful chapters. It's about innocence and that childhood feeling of wanting more and more.

When we are in love big problems suddenly seem small and you catch yourself laughing or smiling for no apparent reason.

Enjoy being in love. Make it last. Discover yourself and discover the one you love. Bring out your inner child for it is when we are children that we love with purity, with intensity and without fear.

Take good care of yourself with these dishes that are welcoming, mothering, feel-good dishes. Start with a soup to warm the heart. Next, a succulent meat dish along with some classic vegetable accompaniments. Risotto, polenta or gnocchi signal it's time to shine. Finish with a delicate dessert, a platter of fruit and cheese and a glass of wine – after all, you're an adult now.

And so now, off to the kitchen. Let that soup bubble, dress the table, light the candles and let the aroma of love invade the world.

500 g (1 lb 2 oz) plain
(all-purpose) flour
15 g (½ oz) fresh yeast or
1½ teaspoons dried yeast
150 g (5½ oz) lard, chopped
3 teaspoons salt
200 g (7 oz) blanched almonds,
chopped
Rosemary leaves, for sprinkling,
optional

Serve your *bello* this traditional Neapolitan snack with a Campari on ice before you win him over with a home-cooked meal to rival his mother's.

Taralli Napoletani

SAVOURY NEAPOLITAN BISCUITS

Place flour on a work surface and form into a well. Place yeast and 110 ml (3¾ fl oz) water in a bowl and stir until dissolved. Pour yeast mixture in centre of well and incorporate a little of the flour. Then add lard, salt and 100 ml (3½ fl oz) of water and mix with the flour until a dough forms. If the dough is a little dry, you may need to add another 1–2 teaspoons water. Knead for about 8 minutes until dough is springy to the touch. Add the almonds and knead for another minute to incorporate. Divide the dough in half, cover with a bowl and rest for 30 minutes.

Preheat oven to 200°C (400°F/Gas 6). Working with one piece of dough at a time and keeping the other piece covered under a bowl, roll each piece until it is about 1 cm (½ in) thick. Cut into 5 cm (2 in) strips. Form a loop from each strip, crossing over the ends, and place on a baking paper-lined oven trays. Sprinkle with freshly ground black pepper and rosemary leaves, if using, and bake for 15 minutes. Reduce heat to 160°C (315°F/Gas 2–3) and bake for 10–15 minutes, then reduce the heat to 130°C (250°F/Gas 1) and bake for 20–30 minutes or until golden and dry.

Serves 6–8

500 g (1 lb 2 oz) plain
(all-purpose) flour
15 g (½ oz) fresh yeast dissolved in
300 ml (10½ fl oz) warm water
2 teaspoons olive oil
Sugo di pomodoro (see p17),
sliced buffalo mozzarella and basil
leaves, to serve

In Italy, Sunday nights are often spent with friends, going out for pizza and beer.
If you don't want to share your *bello*, share this pizza with him at home instead.

Place flour on a work surface and form into a well. Pour yeast mixture and oil in centre
of well and incorporate a little of the flour. Once the mixture has got some consistency, add
2 teaspoons of salt and work in rest of flour to form a dough. Knead for about 10 minutes or
until smooth and elastic. You may need to add a little extra flour if the dough is too sticky.
Cover with a bowl and rest for 2 hours.

Preheat oven to 220°C (425°F/Gas 7). Divide dough in half. Working with one piece of
dough at a time and keeping the other piece covered with a bowl, roll out on a lightly floured
surface until 5 mm (¼ in) thick. Place on lightly oiled oven tray, top with some tomato sauce
and bake for 15 minutes. Remove from oven, add mozzarella and bake for 4–5 minutes or
until just melted. Remove from oven, scatter with fresh basil leaves and serve immediately.

Makes 2 large pizzas

300 g (10½ oz) fresh shelled or dried borlotti beans, if dried soak overnight in cold water
1 litre (35 fl oz/4 cups) beef or vegetable brodo (see p84)
80 ml (2½ fl oz/⅓ cup) olive oil
1 small onion, finely chopped
1 young celery stick with leaves, finely chopped
1 small carrot, finely chopped

150 g (5½ oz) pancetta, chopped
2 pork chops, fat removed
200 g (7 oz) tinned whole tomatoes, puréed
2 bay leaves
150 g (5½ oz) tubetti pasta or other small soup pasta
80 ml (2½ fl oz/⅓ cup) extra virgin olive oil, to serve
Freshly grated parmesan, to serve

Warm your heart and perhaps your lover's soul on a cold winter's night with this deliciously simple soup.

Pasta e Fagioli

PASTA AND BORLOTTI BEAN SOUP

Place beans in a saucepan. If using fresh beans, add the stock, bring to the boil over medium heat, then reduce the heat to low and simmer for 20 minutes or until al dente. Remove from heat and set aside.

If using dried beans, pour in enough cold water to come about 4 fingers above the beans. Bring to the boil over medium heat, then reduce heat to low and simmer for 45 minutes or until tender. Remove from heat and set aside. Drain just before you are ready to use them.

Place olive oil and onion in a heavy-based saucepan over medium heat and cook for 5 minutes or until soft. Add the celery and cook for 2 minutes. Then add the carrot and cook for another 2 minutes. Add the pancetta and cook, stirring, for 3 minutes, then add the pork chops and cook, stirring occasionally, for 10 minutes. Add the stock, beans, tomato and bay leaves, bring to the boil, then reduce the heat to low and simmer gently for 20 minutes.

Once cooked, process two ladlefuls of soup in a food processor. Return puréed soup to the pan and cook for another 10 minutes. Remove the pork chops, coarsely chop the meat and return to the pan. Season and add a little water or stock to thin the soup as you will need to cook the pasta. Bring to a steady moderate boil, add the pasta and cook until al dente. Serve drizzled with extra virgin olive oil and grated parmesan.

Serves 4–6

400 g (14 oz) dried chickpeas, soaked overnight in cold water
200 g (7 oz) pancetta, chopped
2 sprigs rosemary
4 sage leaves
4 garlic cloves, 2 bruised and 2 finely chopped
150 ml (5 fl oz) extra virgin olive oil, plus extra to brush and serve
1 onion, finely chopped

1 handful flat-leaf (Italian) parsley, chopped
2 small red chillies, seeded and finely chopped or a pinch of dried chilli flakes
8 ripe tomatoes, peeled and seeded, or 600 g (1 lb 5 oz) tinned whole tomatoes, puréed
1 litre (35 fl oz/4 cups) vegetable brodo (see p84)
6 slices crusty Italian bread
1 garlic clove, extra, halved

This is another family favourite. I was brought up eating this Tuscan *zuppa* and I can still remember the flavours of my Mamma's cooking, so vivid in my memory. This satisfying *zuppa* is perfect for introducing 'home' food to your loved one.

Zuppa di Ceci

CHICKPEA SOUP

Drain and rinse chickpeas, place in a large heavy-based saucepan and pour in enough cold water to come about 4 fingers above the chickpeas. Add the pancetta, rosemary, sage and bruised garlic cloves and bring to the boil over high heat. Reduce heat to low, cover and simmer for 45 minutes–1 hour or until chickpeas are al dente. You may need to add a little more water.

Place the olive oil in a separate large saucepan over low heat. Add the onion, and cook for 3 minutes. Then add the finely chopped garlic, parsley and chilli, if using, and cook for 5 minutes or until onion is translucent. Add the tomatoes and cook for 25–30 minutes or until thickened and reduced.

Remove chickpeas and pancetta from pan with a slotted spoon and add to tomato mixture. Cook for 10 minutes, then add stock and simmer for 20 minutes. Season to taste. If you prefer a smoother consistency, purée the soup.

Rub bread slices with the cut half of the extra garlic and brush with olive oil and cook under a hot grill (broiler) until golden. Place a slice of bread in each serving bowl, top with soup and serve drizzled with extra olive oil.

Serves 6

400 g (14 oz) dried borlotti beans, soaked in cold water overnight
2 sprigs rosemary
2 bay leaves
500 g (1 lb 2 oz) cotiche or 1 kg (2 lb 4 oz) pork ribs
2 tablespoons extra virgin olive oil, plus extra to serve

1 onion, finely chopped
1 young celery stick with leaves, finely chopped
1 carrot, finely chopped
400 g (14 oz) tinned whole tomatoes, puréed
1.5 litres (52 fl oz/6 cups) vegetable brodo, plus 1 cup extra (see p84)

This is not just another bean soup. Nourishing and richly flavoured, it's comfort food at its best. Cotiche is the end of the leg of a prosciutto with the skin and bone.

Minestra di Cotiche e Fagioli

COTICHE AND BEAN SOUP

Drain beans, place in a heavy-based saucepan and pour in enough cold water to come to about 4 fingers above the beans. Add rosemary, bay leaves and cotiche and simmer over low heat for 40 minutes or until beans are tender. Drain, then when cool enough to handle, peel the cotiche and chop the meat.

If using pork ribs, place the ribs in a saucepan of cold salted water and bring to the boil over high heat. Reduce heat to low and simmer for 1½ hours or until tender. Drain, coarsely chop the meat and set aside.

Place olive oil in a large frying pan over medium heat. Add onion and cook for 5 minutes or until translucent. Add celery and leaves and cook for 2 minutes. Add carrot and cook for 2 minutes. Add chopped meat and cook for 2 minutes. Season to taste. Add tomatoes, stock and drained beans and cook for a further 20 minutes. If soup is too thin, remove 1 ladleful and process in a food processor until smooth, then stir into soup to thicken. If soup is too thick, add extra cup of stock. Check seasoning. Serve drizzled with olive oil.

Serves 6

2½ tablespoons extra virgin olive oil
50 g (1¾ oz) unsalted butter
1.5 kg (3 lb 5 oz) pork neck
2 small onions, sliced
1 small fennel bulb, including
stalks and fronds,
thinly sliced
150 ml (5 fl oz) white wine
150 ml (5 fl oz) vegetable stock
(see p84)

Slow cooking the pork makes it meltingly tender. This hearty dish is for those nights when the pressure is off, when it's all about being comfortable and relaxed.

Maiale al Finocchio

PORK WITH FENNEL

Place half the olive oil and half the butter in a large heavy-based casserole over medium heat and, when hot, add the pork and sear the meat, turning, for about 8 minutes or until brown on all sides. Remove pork from pan and set aside. Discard the oil and butter but do not wash the pan. Add the remaining olive oil and butter and onion. Cook over medium heat for 3 minutes, then add the fennel. Cook for a further 5 minutes, then add the pork. Add wine and cook until evaporated and the strong smell of alcohol has gone. Add stock and season to taste. Cook covered for about 2 hours on a very low heat until pork is tender. Serve with seasonal vegetables.

Serves 6

4 veal cutlets, trimmed by
the butcher
2 eggs
Juice of 1 lemon
100 g (3½ oz/1 cup) dry
breadcrumbs
60 g (2¼ oz) unsalted butter
Lemon wedges, to serve

If you want to impress someone with a special meal, you can't go wrong with this classic Milanese way of preparing veal.

Cotolette alla Milanese

CRUMBED VEAL CUTLETS

Place 1 veal cutlet on a chopping board, cover with plastic wrap then pound with a meat mallet to tenderise. Repeat with the remaining cutlets.

Lightly beat the eggs in a shallow bowl, then add the lemon juice and season to taste. Place breadcrumbs in another shallow bowl. Dip veal cutlets into beaten egg, shaking off excess, then into breadcrumbs, coating well all over.

Place butter in a large frying pan over medium heat and when butter begins to foam, add the cutlets and cook for 4–5 minutes on each side or until cooked through and golden. Remove from pan and drain on paper towels.

Serve immediately with lemon wedges and seasonal vegetables.

Serves 4

Light of Lucia Innamorata Falling in love

8 slices stale bread
8 small ripe tomatoes,
roughly chopped
1 large handful basil leaves, torn
160 ml (5¼ fl oz) extra
virgin olive oil

This is my father's panzanella and his gift to my sister Mirella and me. We have always loved it. We learnt to make it as teenagers and we prepared it as often as possible: as a last-minute meal before bed, or as a comforting supper after a long night of dancing. While preparing it, we would sit and talk and gossip before going to bed, feeling happy and contented.

Panzanella di Peppe

TOMATO AND BREAD SALAD

Dip the bread slices in a bowl of cold water very briefly being careful not to soak the bread. Shake off any excess water. Place in a serving bowl. Add the tomato, basil and olive oil, season generously and toss to combine. Stand for a few minutes before serving.

Serves 4

Light of Lucia Innamorata Falling in love

4 small eggplants (aubergines)
sea salt, for sprinkling
2½ tablespoons extra virgin
olive oil
2 garlic cloves, bruised
1 handful flat-leaf (Italian)
parsley, chopped

Eggplants aren't often used as a side dish but if you love them, this is a quick and easy way to include them in the meal you're preparing. This works just as well with zucchini (courgette).

Melanzane Trifolate

SAUTÉED EGGPLANT

Cut the eggplants into small cubes and place in a colander. Sprinkle generously with sea salt and set aside for at least 30 minutes. Rinse eggplant thoroughly and dry with a cloth.

Place olive oil and garlic in a large frying pan over medium heat and cook for 1 minute, then add the eggplant and stir for 10–12 minutes or until golden and tender.

Remove garlic, season place in a serving dish, scatter with parsley and serve immediately.

Serves 8 as a side dish

1 tablespoon extra virgin olive oil
20 g (¾ oz) unsalted butter
2 onions, finely chopped
2 tomatoes, seeded and chopped
600 g (1 lb 5 oz/about 2 bunches)
English spinach, leaves picked
and washed
4 eggs
Freshly grated parmesan, to serve

A quick dish for days when you have no time or inclination to cook. For a richer, more elegant version, make a quick béchamel and mix it through the spinach.

SPINACH WITH EGGS

Place olive oil and butter in a wide, deep frying pan over low heat, add the onion and cook for 5 minutes or until onion is translucent. Add the tomato and cook for another 3 minutes, then add the spinach and stir until wilted, (if necessary, remove some of the excess water released by the spinach). Season and remove from heat. Flatten spinach out in pan and, using a tablespoon, make 4 small wells in the spinach. Crack an egg into each well. Return to heat and cook, covered, until eggs have set. Sprinkle with parmesan and serve.

Serves 4

Note To make eggs florentine, a richer, oven-baked version of this recipe, finish a béchamel sauce (see p63) with parmesan and a little nutmeg, then combine with the cooked spinach and place in a shallow oven-proof dish. Once again, make little wells in the spinach, crack an egg into each one, then bake at 200°C (400°F/Gas 6) for 15 minutes or until the eggs are just set.

200 ml (7 fl oz) extra virgin olive oil

4 desiree potatoes, cut into cubes

3 red capsicums (peppers), seeded, membrane removed and cut into strips

3 eggplants (aubergines), cut into cubes

1 large onion, finely chopped

2 garlic cloves, finely chopped

3 tomatoes, peeled, seeded and chopped

2 teaspoons finely chopped oregano, plus extra to serve

1 small handful flat-leaf (Italian) parsley finely chopped

Thyme sprigs, to serve

This is one of my Mamma's best recipes. She would make it all the time, using whatever vegetables she had on hand. Try it as a side dish or as an antipasto.

Ciamfotta

MY MAMMA'S SPECIAL VEGETABLE DISH

Heat 50 ml (1½ fl oz) olive oil in a large heavy-based frying pan over medium heat. When hot, add potato and cook, stirring, until golden and tender. Remove with a slotted spoon, season to taste and set aside.

Add 50 ml (1½ fl oz) olive oil to the pan and, when hot, add capsicum and cook, stirring, until soft. Remove with a slotted spoon, season to taste and set aside.

Add 50 ml (1½ fl oz) olive oil to the pan and, when hot, add eggplant and cook, stirring, until golden and tender. Remove, season to taste and set aside when hot.

Add 50 ml (1½ fl oz) olive oil to the pan and when hot, add onion and cook for 3 minutes or until soft, then add garlic and cook for 2 minutes. Add tomato, reduce heat to low and simmer for 10 minutes or until thickened and reduced. Stir in oregano and parsley and season to taste. Then add all cooked vegetables to tomato sauce and cook, stirring gently, for 3–5 minutes or until heated through. Serve scattered with thyme sprigs and extra oregano.

Serves 8

170 g (6 oz) unsalted butter,
chopped, plus extra for greasing
110 g (3¾ oz) plain (all-purpose)
flour, sifted, plus extra for dusting
200 g (7 oz) dark chocolate
(minimum 50 per cent cocoa)
4 large eggs
100 g (3½ oz) caster (superfine) sugar
60 ml (2 fl oz/¼ cup)
freshly made espresso, cooled

Watch the chocolate ooze from these exquisite little treats as you break them
with a spoon. Cook them for exactly 8 minutes or they will lose the ooze. Who
could resist this dish or its cook?

Tortino di Cioccolato

LITTLE CHOCOLATE CAKES

Preheat oven to 220°C (425°F/Gas 7). Lightly butter and flour six 125 ml (4 fl oz/½ cup)
capacity ramekins or moulds. Place chocolate and butter in a heatproof bowl set over a
saucepan of simmering water. Stir until melted, then set aside to cool. Place eggs and sugar
in a bowl and beat with electric beaters for 6–8 minutes or until thick and pale. Gently fold
flour into egg mixture, then fold in cooled chocolate mixture, followed by the espresso. Divide
between prepared ramekins and bake for 8 minutes. Invert onto serving plates or serve in
the ramekins if you wish.

Serves 6

2 large eggs, separated
50 g (1¾ oz) caster sugar
150 g (5½ oz) mascarpone
30 g (1 oz) dark chocolate
50 ml (1½ fl oz) Nocino liqueur
or Frangelico
whipped cream, to serve (optional)

If you're cooking dinner with seduction in mind, a lot rests on dessert.
This mascarpone cream is a winner, for its simplicity of preparation and
its memorable taste.

Mascarpone al Nocino

MASCARPONE WITH WALNUT LIQUEUR

Place egg yolks and sugar in a bowl and beat with an electric beater for about 7 minutes or
until thick and pale, Add mascarpone and fold in gently until just combined.

In a separate bowl, beat the egg whites until stiff peaks form. Then fold gently into the
mascarpone mixture.

Meanwhile, place the chocolate in a heatproof bowl and set over a saucepan of simmering
water. Stir until melted, then remove from heat and add the liqueur.

Divide half the chocolate mixture between 4 tall glasses, top with half of the mascarpone
mixture, then repeat. Refrigerate for 1 hour before serving with whipped cream, if desired.

Serves 4

4 large eggs, separated
100 g (3½ oz) caster (superfine) sugar
500 g (1 lb 2 oz) mascarpone
100 ml (3½ fl oz) marsala or
medium dry sherry or brandy
(if using brandy, dilute with water)

300 ml (10½ fl oz) freshly made
espresso, cooled and
slightly sweetened
Savoiardi biscuits or 1 sponge cake
Unsweetened cocoa powder

This is one of the best tiramisù recipes I have come across. There are many variations out there but you must promise me to use mascarpone, and mascarpone only. I find it has much better flavour if it has been refrigerated for at least one day before serving.

Tiramisù

Place egg yolks and sugar in a bowl and beat with electric beaters until thick and pale. Gently stir in mascarpone. Beat the egg whites in a separate bowl until stiff peaks form, then gently fold into mascarpone mixture.

Place marsala in a shallow bowl with 125 ml (4 fl oz/½ cup) of water. Pour coffee in a shallow bowl. Dip enough savoiardi biscuits into coffee to cover the base of a baking paper-lined 25 cm (10 in) springform cake tin. Be careful that you do not oversoak the biscuits. This is the secret. Top with half of the mascarpone mixture and sprinkle with cocoa powder. Top with another layer of biscuits, this time dipped in the marsala and top with remaining mascarpone mixture. Chill in the refrigerator for at least 4 hours or preferably overnight before serving. Just before serving, remove cake tin and sprinkle generously with cocoa powder.

Serves 8

6

Matrimonio

È arrivato il gran giorno.
Tradizioni e superstizioni
nel matrimonio.

Wedding day
It's Lucia's big day. A wedding is the most beautiful celebration in Italy
and there are many customs and superstitions that help mark the occasion.

"Today is your big day," said Nonna. "Your wedding day."

The celebrations started a few months earlier but today we can talk, we can cherish the moment and we can enjoy this great success.

Both families unite to celebrate a new chapter. As part of the ritual, certain superstitious beliefs need to be attended to, becoming part of the story we will carry in our hearts. Ribbons are stretched across the top of church doorways and a shower of confetti covers the couple as they enter the piazza to greet their loved ones.

"I wonder do things change or do they remain the same?" Nonna asked me, recalling the traditions she enjoyed on her own wedding day. "You get a new kitchen with big pots for cooking plenty of pasta and so did I on my wedding day."

As wishes for good luck, five sugar-covered almonds tied in a little bag (bomboniere) – one for each guest – are placed on each table, representing fertility, wealth and prosperity.

"Luck is all we need for you Lucia so I will wear green just before the big day," said Nonna. "And I will make some bow ties on your wedding day. That is right… farfalle and little candies twisted into knots and all the family will be together.

"Ah," said Nonna, "I will drop a glass that will break into many pieces and those pieces will signify how many years of happiness you will enjoy. We always need a bit of luck here."

And as with all Italian weddings, expect a long lunch or dinner that will last a few hours or even a few days. And for your special guests, give away a booklet of your family's recipes like the ones I have chosen here.

12 figs
100 ml (3½ fl oz) milk
100 g (3½ oz) gorgonzola dolce,
chopped
12 slices prosciutto

My friend Enrico's mum, a Neapolitan, instilled in him a love for cooking and blending incredible flavours. She has given this wonderful man 'the touch'. And a love of perfection.

Fichi di Enrico

ENRICO'S FIGS WITH GORGONZOLA AND PROSCIUTTO

Peel the figs and trim bases flat to ensure they sit upright on a plate. Trim the stems, then cut a cross on top of each fig.

Place milk in a saucepan over medium heat and, when hot, add the gorgonzola and stir until melted. Remove from heat.

Wrap each fig in a slice of prosciutto. Place on a serving platter and, just before serving, top each one with 1 tablespoon of warm gorgonzola sauce. Serve immediately.

Serves 6

1 tablespoon olive oil
30 g (1 oz) unsalted butter
4 garlic cloves, bruised
12 walnuts, coarsely crushed
1 tablespoon plain (all-purpose)
flour, sifted
250 ml (9 fl oz/1 cup) hot milk
1 quantity pasta fresca, cut into
tagliatelle (see p54)
Freshly grated parmesan, to serve

This is a beautiful way to coat tagliatelle as they do it in Emilia with a béchamel base they call *salsa vellutata*. In Liguria they make their walnut sauce using a mortar and pestle as they would make their famous pesto.

Tagliatelle alle Noci

PASTA WITH WALNUT SAUCE

Place olive oil, butter and garlic in a frying pan over low heat and cook for 2 minutes or until garlic is golden. Remove garlic. Add walnuts and cook, stirring for 3 minutes, then remove pan from heat. Add flour and stir vigorously until well combined. Return the pan to the heat and after 1 minute, gradually add the hot milk, whisking continuously until nice and smooth. After 2 minutes check the sauce for seasoning. This is a very velvety sauce and does not have the same consistency as a béchamel, hence the name vellutata – a much more liquid béchamel.

Cook pasta in plenty of boiling salted water until al dente. With a slotted spoon or *mandolino* (see glossary), remove some of the pasta and place in a bowl. Start adding the sauce to the pasta, stirring so it will be well coated and not stick. Continue to remove the pasta, adding the sauce and stirring until all the pasta is removed and coated in sauce. Serve immediately with parmesan.

Serves 4

20 g (¾ oz) unsalted butter
1 onion, finely chopped
2 x 400 g (14 oz) tinned whole
tomatoes, puréed
250 ml (9 fl oz/1 cup) milk
1 quantity pasta fresca (see p54)
Freshly grated parmesan, to serve
Chopped flat-leaf (Italian)
parsley, to serve

Filling
8 marinated artichoke hearts,
drained
1 small handful flat-leaf (Italian)
parsley, finely chopped
1 egg
150 g (5½ oz) grated parmesan

I had this beautiful pasta dish at a friend's house in Italy. As I returned home
I rushed to the kitchen to replicate this beautiful recipe.

Tortelli di Carciofi

ARTICHOKE TORTELLI

To make filling Place all ingredients in a food processor and process until well combined.
Place in a bowl, cover with plastic wrap and refrigerate for 4 hours or overnight.

Place butter in a saucepan over medium heat, add onion and cook for 5 minutes or until
onion is translucent. Add tomatoes and bring to the boil. Reduce the heat to low, add milk
and simmer for 1 hour or until thickened and reduced. Don't worry if sauce curdles, it will
return to normal after 20 minutes of cooking. Remove from heat and season.

To make tortelli, follow instructions on page 54 for making pasta fresca. Work with only
1 piece of dough at a time, and keep the remaining dough covered with a bowl until you're
ready to put it through the pasta machine. Place tablespoons of filling 2 cm (¾ in) up from
the bottom of a pasta sheet and 5 cm (2 in) apart. Fold over the top half of the pasta sheet to
enclose filling. Press between filling to remove air pockets, then press the edges to seal well.
Using a pastry wheel cutter, cut tortelli into squares or semicircles. Place tortelli on a clean
tea towel (dish towel) sprinkled with flour and place in front of a fan to dry. Repeat with
remaining dough.

Cook tortelli in plenty of boiling salted water until they rise to the surface and are al dente.
Remove with a slotted spoon, place in serving bowl and toss gently with prepared sauce.
Sprinkle with parsley and serve immediately with parmesan.

Serves 4

2 kg (4 lb 8 oz) rabbit, cut
into 8 pieces
80 ml (2½ fl oz/⅓ cup) olive oil
3 sprigs rosemary
3 garlic cloves, bruised
400 ml (14 fl oz) white wine

20 g (¾ oz) unsalted butter
250 ml (9 fl oz/1 cup) hot
vegetable brodo (see p84)
150 ml (5 fl oz) balsamic vinegar
50 g (1¾ oz) brown sugar

The balsamic vinegar really flavours the rabbit, transforming it into something else altogether. You need to start this recipe the night before.

Coniglio all' Aceto

RABBIT WITH BALSAMIC VINEGAR

Place rabbit pieces in a bowl, add 2 tablespoons of the olive oil, rosemary, garlic and wine, combine well, cover with plastic wrap and refrigerate overnight.

Preheat oven to 200°C (400°F/Gas 6). Drain rabbit, reserving marinade, and pat dry with paper towel. Place butter and remaining oil in a large heavy-based frying pan over medium heat, add rabbit and cook until browned on all sides.

Place rabbit in a roasting tin, pour over reserved marinade and roast for 15 minutes. Check rabbit and if it looks a little dry, add a ladleful of stock. Remove rabbit from the oven.

Meanwhile, place vinegar in a small saucepan and bring to the boil over medium heat. Cook for 2 minutes, then add sugar and cook, stirring, until sugar dissolves and mixture becomes syrupy, about 15 minutes. Taste it and, if necessary, add a little more sugar – it should have a light syrupy flavour. Pour over rabbit and return to the oven and cook for another 15 minutes. Rest for 10 minutes before serving with seasonal vegetables.

Serves 4

750 ml (26 fl oz/3 cups) milk
or enough to cover the veal
2 tablespoons extra virgin olive oil
50 g (1¾ oz) unsalted butter
800 g (1 lb 12 oz) boneless
veal shoulder
1 handful each rosemary and sage leaves
Warm spiced pears, to serve
(recipe overleaf)

This dish represents the north of Italy at its best. Delicately flavoured with milk and sage, it is simple, rustic and delicious. The milk will coagulate but don't worry, as you sieve, this coagulation will disappear and you will be left with a beautifully flavoured silky sauce.

Vitello al Latte

VEAL WITH MILK

Place the milk in a saucepan and bring to the boil. Remove from heat and set aside.

Place olive oil and half of the butter in a large heavy-based saucepan over medium heat until the butter has melted. Increase the heat to high, then add the veal and cook, turning often, until browned on all sides. Remove veal and set aside.

Discard all the fat from the pan and wipe pan clean with a paper towel. Add remaining butter to the pan over medium heat, add rosemary and sage leaves, stir for 1–2 minutes, then return meat to pan and cook for 5 minutes to absorb flavours. Add boiled milk, reduce heat to low and simmer with the lid slightly ajar for 1½ hours or until meat is tender. Remove veal from pan and place on a serving platter. Rest for 15 minutes.

Meanwhile strain the milk sauce through a fine sieve, pour over the veal and serve with warm spiced pears.

Serves 4

575 g (1 lb 4½ oz/2½ cups)
caster (superfine) sugar
2 cinnamon sticks,
broken into pieces
4 cloves
2 large lemons, sliced
4 firm William pears, peeled,
with stalks attached

These pears are delicious served with veal cooked in milk (see p232) – you can leave them whole or purée them. They also work well served with cheeses, cold meats and pâté. If you like, you can substitute the William pears with Granny Smith apples.

Pere alle Spezie

WARM SPICED PEARS

Place sugar, spices, lemon slices and 625 ml (21½ fl oz/2½ cups) of water in a heavy-based saucepan and stir over a low heat until the sugar dissolves. Add the pears and simmer for 30 minutes or until just tender. Drain and serve warm.

Serves 4 as a side dish

6 blood oranges
4 young celery sticks with leaves,
sticks thinly sliced,
leaves finely chopped
80 ml (2½ fl oz/⅓ cup) extra
virgin olive oil

If you can't find blood oranges for this beautiful Sicilian salad, then it's best to give this dish a miss. It is also delicious scattered with thinly sliced fennel and chopped fennel fronds.

Insalata di Arance

ORANGE SALAD

Peel the oranges including white pith. Cut them into 5 mm (¼ in) thick rounds. Place the oranges on a serving platter and scatter with the celery and leaves. Just before serving, drizzle with olive oil, season and serve immediately.

Serves 4

Light of Lucia Matrimonio Wedding day

200 ml (7 fl oz) thickened cream
200 ml (7 fl oz) milk
150 g (5½ oz) dark chocolate,
chopped
150 g (5½ oz) caster (superfine) sugar
1 gelatine leaf (titanium strength)
2 large eggs
30 ml (1 fl oz) Cognac

Italian children are brought up eating *budino*. This grown-up version, spiced with a little Cognac, is for special occasions. It's rich and decadent yet comfortingly familiar.

Budino di Cioccolato con Salsa al Caramello

CHOCOLATE PUDDINGS WITH CARAMEL SAUCE

Place cream, milk, chocolate and half the sugar in a saucepan over medium heat and stir until the chocolate is melted and the mixture is well combined. Remove from heat and set aside to cool. Stir eggs, one at a time, into the cooled chocolate mixture, then stir in Cognac. Place the gelatine leaf in a bowl, cover with cold water and soak for 2–3 minutes. Squeeze excess water from gelatine leaf and add to chocolate mixture. Return mixture to medium heat and bring just to the boil, stirring continuously. Whisk to ensure the mixture is smooth then remove from the heat.

Grease eight 125 ml (4 fl oz/½ cup)–capacity ramekins. Place 2 tablespoons of water and the remaining sugar in a small, heavy-based saucepan and stir over low heat until sugar dissolves. Simmer, without stirring, until a dark caramel forms, being careful not to burn it. Working quickly, pour a little caramel into each ramekin, turning to coat base and side. Divide chocolate mixture between ramekins (they will be about three-quarters full) and refrigerate for at least 3 hours or until set. Just before serving, place ramekins in an oven tray filled with boiling water for 2 minutes, then carefully run a knife inside each ramekin and invert onto serving plates.

Serves 8

7

La Suocera

Ricordati che la forza cresce nel giardino della pazienza. E la suocera è una sfida. Anche in cucina.

Mother-in-law

Ah, the challenges of having a mother-in-law, especially in the kitchen. Invite her over for Sunday lunches and learn her secrets and traditions.

Like any Italian girl, marriage means sharing: sharing family, Sundays, and your life. Balance the gossip and try to be the perfect mother in the eyes of the in-laws. Most of all appear calm and elegant at all times.

"You must learn this fast, Lucia," whispered my Nonna. "Never compete with the mother of your loved one. This is the woman who carried him for so long. She fed him, she gave up many nights, she taught him to read and write, she prepared his favourite food and has always hidden the recipes. This is not because she is vicious; it's because she doesn't want to lose him."

The mother-in-law is proud of her roots and her recipes will represent her home region. She will always tell you how hard she worked but her recipes she will never share. The mother insists on being the best and this should not be put to the test. Impress her with your own cooking but don't compete with her recipes. Choose a dish from a region different to where she's from.

In this chapter, you will discover the secret recipes of each region for you to cook for your mother-in-law.

Here also is a bread and not any simple bread. This is a bread that will deliver its flavours in three days and three nights.

Enjoy the challenges that lie ahead. Simplicity is hard to master so now is the time: learn to make *pappa al pomodoro* instantly, although you need a lifetime to master the flavours. Silly are those who think they can learn overnight. To master anything – from making a dish to controlling your feelings – you need time.

Remember life for the old Italians was about survival. So, of course, they are proud. Enjoy these last pages of their treasured recipes.

125 ml (4 fl oz/½ cup) extra virgin olive oil, plus extra to serve
3 large onions, finely chopped
500 g (1 lb 2 oz) ripe tomatoes, peeled, seeded and chopped
1 handful basil leaves, torn
1 handful young celery leaves, chopped

1.5 litres (52 fl oz/6 cups) vegetable stock (see p84) or water
6 eggs
6 slices stale Italian bread
grated Pecorino Toscano or parmesan, to serve

Literally meaning cooked water, *aquacotta* was the food of poor people. It was for people who worked hard in the woods or travelled from town to town. And it was created from the foods they would find along the way. Sometimes it was mushrooms, other times a shepherd would swap a piece of cheese for an egg. So it's not surprising there are many different versions of *aquacotta*. This humble dish warmed their hearts and souls.

Acquacotta di Maremma

PEASANT SOUP FROM MAREMMA

Place olive oil in a large wide saucepan over low heat. Add the onion and cook for 5 minutes or until translucent. Add the tomato, basil and celery leaves and simmer for about 20 minutes or until thickened. Add stock, increase heat to medium and bring to the boil, then reduce heat to low and simmer for 40 minutes.

Just before serving, crack the eggs, one at a time, into a ramekin or cup and gently slide into the soup. Cover the pan and cook just until the eggs are done to your liking. Remove soup from heat.

Place a slice of bread in each bowl, top with soup, being careful that you do not break the eggs and giving each person one egg. Sprinkle with Pecorino Toscano and serve with a drizzle of olive oil.

Serves 6

Light of Lucia La suocera Mother-in-law

2½ tablespoons extra virgin olive oil,
A pinch of dried chilli flakes
1 handful flat-leaf parsley,
finely chopped

Gnocchi
1 kg (2 lb 4 oz) desiree potatoes,
unpeeeled
200 g (7 oz) plain (all-purpose)
flour, plus a little extra

Leek sauce
1 tablespoon extra virgin olive oil
2 leeks, finely sliced
50 g (1¾ oz) toasted walnuts,
chopped
50 g (1¾ oz) ricotta salata
(see glossary) or parmesan,
grated

The Tuscans call these delicate little gnocchi *topini*, little mice. Before making the entire batch, test a couple of gnocchi by cooking in boiling salted water.

Topini ai Porri

LITTLE GNOCCHI WITH LEEKS

Pour the oil into a bowl and stir in chilli and parsley. Set aside to infuse flavours.

To make gnocchi Bring a large saucepan of salted water to the boil. Place potatoes in another large saucepan of cold salted water and simmer until tender. Drain, peel and put through a potato ricer, making a pile of mash on a floured surface. Cool completely, add a large pinch of salt and sift flour over, leaving about 50 g (1¾ oz) of flour aside. Mix with your hands to form a smooth dough. Divide into quarters and roll into cylinders 1 cm (½ in) in diameter. Break a small piece from one of the cylinders and cut into 1.5 cm (⅝ in)–long pieces, then make an indentation in each with your index finger and roll it on the bench. Drop the test-topini into the boiling water to see if they hold their shape. If they collapse, you'll need to add a little of the remaining flour to the dough cylinders. If they are fine, cut the cylinders into pieces and repeat the indenting and rolling process as above. Place topini on a floured tray, cover with a tea towel (dish towel) and rest for 30 minutes.

To make leek sauce Place oil in a large frying pan over low heat, add leeks and a little water. Cook for 10 minutes or until tender and water has evaporated. Stir in walnuts. Remove from heat.

Cook the gnocchi in batches in boiling salted water; when they rise to the surface, let them cook for 1 minute more then remove with a slotted spoon. Place in a serving bowl and toss with the chilli-parsley oil and leek sauce. Serve sprinkled with ricotta salata.

Serves 6

50 g (1¾ oz) unsalted butter
2 tablespoons olive oil
1 kg (2 lb 4 oz) beef rump steak
or veal shoulder, trimmed and cut
into 4 cm (1½ in) pieces
250 ml (9 fl oz/1 cup) Chianti or
other red wine
1 garlic bulb

3 teaspoons coarsely ground
black pepper
1 tablespoon tomato paste
(concentrated purée) mixed
with 50 ml (1½ fl oz) hot water
2 cloves
5 juniper berries, optional
Polenta, to serve

The story goes that four million tiles were needed to finish a magnificent cathedral in Florence. This dish – slowly cooked meat with wine and pepper – was created to feed the hungry men who worked on this project. At the time, pepper was a way of preserving meat. The workers enjoyed this dish between shifts, with a glass of Chianti.

PEPPERED BEEF

Preheat oven to 160°C (315°F/Gas 2–3). Place butter and oil in a heavy-based casserole over medium heat and, when hot, cook the meat in batches until browned all over. Add the remaining ingredients (except polenta) and just enough water to cover the meat. Bring to the boil, then cover with a lid or foil and bake in oven, stirring occasionally, for about 3 hours or until meat is very tender and sauce has thickened – you may have to add more water while cooking. Remove meat and strain sauce, discarding solids. Serve peppered beef on polenta or cooked vegetables, topped with the sauce.

Serves 6

500 g (1 lb 2 oz) cooked spinach
(about 1 kg/2 lb 4 oz uncooked),
squeezed to remove water
300 g (10½ oz) ricotta
2 eggs, lightly beaten
2 tablespoons plain (all-purpose)
flour, plus a little extra

Freshly grated nutmeg, to taste
125 g (4½ oz) unsalted butter
1 handful sage leaves
Freshly grated parmesan, to serve

A classic Tuscan dish, these delicate little *gnudi* or dumplings require a watchful eye – too little flour and they may fall apart, too much flour and you'll get dumplings heavy enough to incur the wrath of your mother-in-law!

SPINACH AND RICOTTA DUMPLINGS

Bring a large saucepan of water to the boil. Place the squeezed spinach in a food processor and finely chop. Transfer to a large bowl with the ricotta and combine well. Mix in the eggs and flour, season and add nutmeg to taste. Using 2 spoons, shape 1 tablespoon of mixture into a dumpling and drop into boiling water to see if it holds its shape when cooked. If not, add a little of the extra flour to the mixture.

When you are ready to serve, return water to the boil, adding plenty of salt. Shape the mixture into dumplings as before and drop, in batches, in boiling water. As soon as dumplings float to the surface, cook for 1 minute, then remove with a slotted spoon and place in a shallow serving bowl.

Place butter and sage in a small saucepan and cook over medium heat until butter is melted and bubbling and sage is crisp. Pour over the *gnudi* and serve sprinkled with parmesan.

Serves 6

Light of Lucia La suocera Mother-in-law

4 eggplants (aubergines), firm
but not too hard
150 ml (5 fl oz) extra
virgin olive oil
2 eggs, lightly beaten
100 g (3½ oz/1 cup) dry
breadcrumbs
200 g (7 oz/2 cups) grated parmesan

1 handful flat-leaf (Italian) parsley,
finely chopped
4 garlic cloves, finely chopped
1 onion, finely chopped
2 x 400 g (14 oz) tinned whole
tomatoes, puréed
1 handful basil leaves, roughly
torn, plus extra to serve

My Nonna, Giulia, came from Sapri, which is south of the Amalfi Coast. This is
her delicious version of stuffed eggplant.

Melanzane Ripiene

STUFFED EGGPLANT

Cut the eggplants in half lengthways. Using a metal spoon, scoop the flesh out of each half and
cut into small cubes. Cut two slits lengthways into the skin side of the hollowed halves (these
slits are necessary so that the eggplant will cook well in the sauce).

Place 2½ tablespoons olive oil in a non-stick frying pan over high heat. Add cubed eggplant
flesh and cook, stirring occasionally, for 10 minutes or until golden and tender. Season to taste,
then remove from heat and set aside to cool.

Place eggs, breadcrumbs, parmesan, parsley, half the garlic and the cooled eggplant in
a bowl. Mix until well combined (it should be the consistency of pâté) and season to taste.
Divide filling between the eggplant halves, smoothing top with a knife.

Place 1 tablespoon oil in a large frying pan over medium heat and, when hot, cook stuffed
eggplants, in 3 batches, filling side first, for 2 minutes on each side, adding more oil for each batch.

Add remaining 2 tablespoons of oil to pan, add onion and cook over medium heat for
5 minutes or until soft. Add remaining garlic and cook for 2 minutes. Add tomatoes and cook
for 20 minutes. Add the basil and season to taste. Add stuffed eggplants, filled side up, and
cook over low heat for 35 minutes. Serve immediately scattered with extra basil.

Serves 8

Light of Lucia La suocera Mother-in-law

100 ml (3½ fl oz) extra virgin olive
oil, plus extra to serve
3 garlic cloves, finely sliced
1 leek, finely sliced
1 kg (2 lb 4 oz) ripe tomatoes,
peeled, seeded and chopped

1 handful basil leaves, torn
500 ml (17 fl oz/2 cups) vegetable
stock (see p84)
6 slices stale Italian
bread, torn
Freshly grated pecorino toscano
or parmesan, to serve

This dish is the unofficial symbol of Tuscany – if you visit that beautiful region,
you're certain to try it.

Pappa al Pomodoro

SIMPLE TOMATO AND BREAD 'SOUP'

Place olive oil and garlic in a large saucepan over low heat and cook for 1 minute or until
garlic is soft, then add leek and cook for about 10 minutes or until soft. Add the tomatoes and
half the basil, turn heat up to medium and bring to the boil. Reduce heat to low and simmer
for 10 minutes. Add the stock and simmer for 20 minutes. Season to taste, then add bread and
cook for another 3 minutes. Add remaining basil. Cover with a lid, remove from heat and rest
for about 1 hour.

Serve at room temperature or slightly warmed, sprinkled with pecorino toscano and
drizzled with the extra olive oil.

Serves 6

Light of Lucia La suocera Mother-in-law

350 g (12 oz) plain (all-purpose)
flour, sifted
Freshly grated parmesan, to serve

Pesto
50 g (1¾ oz) basil leaves
1 garlic clove, chopped

1½ tablespoons pine nuts, chopped
35 g (1¼ oz) grated parmesan
15 g (½ oz) tablespoons
good-quality grated pecorino
75 ml (2¼ fl oz) extra virgin
olive oil

Every good wife should be able to perfect pesto. The secret is to add a little of the pasta cooking water and never extra oil.

Place flour on a work surface, make a well in the centre, pour 130 ml (4½ fl oz) of water in the centre and incorporate flour from the sides. Knead for 10 minutes or until dough is elastic and smooth, adding more water if dry or more flour if necessary. Cover with a bowl and rest for 30 minutes.

Take a small piece of dough and, using your little finger, roll on a floured surface, pressing on the table and moving your hand up. Then roll again, pressing towards the left until you make fine curly little 'worms' of pasta, known as trofie, which are perfectly designed to catch the pesto. Place on a lightly floured tray in a well ventilated spot to dry.

To make pesto Using scissors cut the basil and place into a mortar with the garlic and pine nuts, add ½ teaspoon of salt and pound with a pestle until a rough paste forms. Add the cheeses and pound until well combined. Transfer to a bowl and slowly add the oil. Alternatively, use a food processor but you'll need to work quickly; it should take seconds, not minutes.

Cook trofie in a large saucepan of boiling salted water until al dente. Drain, reserving cooking water. Place trofie in a bowl and toss with the pesto – adding 2 tablespoons of cooking water for every 1 tablespoon of pesto – until well combined. Serve immediately sprinkled with extra parmesan.

Serves 4

A *piece on* pici

Pici, a regional pasta typically from Val di Chiana, is like spaghetti but much thicker. It is made by rolling the dough between your thumb and index finger.

Pici represents a time of Tuscan struggles, up until half a century ago, when families living in farmhouses had very little comfort and housewives had to use whatever they had in the kitchen.

So they created a pasta, which could feed the many members of their family, made from plain flour and water – and generally no eggs, as these were something they would reserve for Sunday lunch.

But they had olive oil, which was all they needed to grease their hands for rolling the pasta with.

Why is pici in this chapter?

Well, you may want to tell your mother-in-law, how you conquered her son and made him your husband. *Appiccicando*! You stuck on him like glue when you made pici with plenty of love. It's food for thought. And she will forever chew on this tale.

500 g (1 lb 2 oz) plain (all-purpose)
flour, sifted,
plus extra for dusting
Extra virgin olive oil,
for greasing
Freshly grated parmesan, to serve

Pici go well with a good classical *ragù Bolognese* (see p59), as shown here,
or serve it with the sauce and juices from the *peposo* (see p246) or *stracotto*
(see p170) so you have two meals from one.

HAND–ROLLED PASTA

Place all the flour on a work surface and make a well in the centre. Pour 180 ml (5¾ fl oz) of water in the centre and incorporate flour from the sides. Check to see if you need to add any more water or flour. Knead for 10 minutes or until dough is smooth.

Cut the dough in half and, working with one half at a time, keeping the other half covered by a bowl, roll out until 1 cm (½ in) thick, then cut into 1 cm (½ in)–wide strips. Lightly grease your hands with olive oil, then roll each strip, moving your hands back and forth to make long, thin snakes (thick spaghetti shapes). As you make them, place on a lightly floured tray or over a clean broom handle in front of a fan to dry. Repeat with remaining dough.

Cook in batches in plenty of salted boiling water until al dente. Drain, reserving a little of the cooking water, and place in a serving bowl. Add your choice of sauce to the pasta and, if a little dry, add some of the reserved cooking water. Serve immediately sprinkled with parmesan.

Serves 6

600 g (1 lb 5 oz) durum wheat
flour, sifted
600 g (1 lb 5 oz) cime di rapa,
washed and trimmed, or
broccolini, cut into small pieces
100 ml (3½ fl oz) extra virgin
olive oil

2 garlic cloves, finely chopped
A small pinch of dried chilli flakes
4 anchovy fillets, chopped
Fresh breadcrumbs, fried in a
little olive oil until crisp or grated
pecorino or parmesan, to serve

Orecchiette alle Cime di Rapa

ORECCHIETTE WITH CIME DI RAPA

Place a mound of flour on a work surface and make a well in the centre. Pour 250 ml (9 fl oz/ 1 cup) of water into the centre of the well and incorporate flour from the sides. You may need to add a little bit more water or flour to get the right consistency. Knead for 10 minutes or until dough is smooth. Cover with a bowl and rest for 30 minutes.

Divide dough into quarters and work with one quarter at a time, keeping the rest under the bowl. On a lightly floured surface, roll dough back and forth to form a 5 mm (¼ in)–thick strip. Using a table knife, cut each strip into small pieces and press down with the knife to form the orecchiette or you can use your thumb to press down on them to create little 'ears'. Place on a lightly floured tray in front of a fan to dry. Repeat with remaining dough.

Cook orecchiette in boiling salted water. Halfway through cooking, add the cime di rapa. Meanwhile, place olive oil in a large frying pan over low heat, add the garlic, chilli flakes and anchovies and cook, using a wooden spoon to break up anchovies, for 2–3 minutes. Once the pasta is al dente, drain with the greens, reserving cooking water, and add to frying pan, stirring to coat pasta in anchovy sauce. Stir in 2 ladlefuls of reserved cooking water and serve topped with breadcrumbs, pecorino or parmesan.

Serves 6

440 g (15½ oz) durum wheat flour
4 eggs
Freshly grated pecorino, to serve

Ragù

200 ml (7 fl oz) olive oil
1 onion, finely chopped
2 garlic cloves, finely chopped
3 young celery sticks with leaves,
finely chopped

1 carrot, finely chopped
100 g (3½ oz) pancetta, finely chopped
1 kg (2 lb 4 oz) pieces of mixed meat, such
as veal and pork shoulder and chuck steak
150 ml (5 fl oz) red wine
2 x 400 g (14 oz) tinned whole
tomatoes, puréed
2 bay leaves
500 ml (17 fl oz/2 cups) beef brodo (see p84)

A specialty from Abruzzo, this pasta is so-called because the wooden frame strung with wire that is used to make it resembles the neck of a guitar (*chitarra*). The meat is used to flavour the sauce, but can be removed and served as a separate course with vegetables.

FLAT MACCHERONI WITH RAGÙ

To make ragù Place oil in a large heavy-based saucepan, add onion and cook over low heat for 5 minutes or until soft. Add garlic and cook for 1 minute, add celery and leaves, cook for 3 minutes, then add carrot and cook for 3 minutes. Add pancetta and cook for another 3 minutes. Increase heat to high and add meat, turning to brown on all sides. Add wine and cook until evaporated and the smell of alcohol has gone. Add tomato and bay leaves and most of the stock, reduce heat to low and simmer for 2–3 hours, adding remaining stock if necessary, until meat is tender. Season to taste, remove meat from sauce and set aside.

    To make maccheroni Follow instructions on page 54 for making pasta fresca using the weights above. Cut pasta sheets into pieces the same length as the *chitarra*, lay on top of the strings and use a rolling pin to press pasta through the strings. Place on a lightly floured tray in front of a fan to dry or hang over a broom handle. Cook maccheroni in boiling salted water until al dente. Use a *mandolino* (see glossary) or slotted spoon to scoop the maccheroni into a bowl, tossing with the sauce until well combined. Serve immediately sprinkled with pecorino. Serve meat as a separate course with steamed vegetables.

Serves 6

550 g (1 lb 4 oz) type '0' flour
5 eggs

Filling
2 tablespoons extra virgin olive oil
40 g (1½ oz) unsalted butter
½ onion, finely chopped
½ young celery stick, finely
chopped and leaves reserved
½ carrot, finely chopped
100 g (3½ oz) veal shoulder

100 g (3½ oz) chuck steak
100 g (3½ oz) pork shoulder
150 ml (5 fl oz) white wine
1 tablespoon tomato paste
(concentrated purée)
5 litres (175 fl oz) unstrained
brodo (see p84)
2 eggs, lightly beaten
350 g (12 oz) grated parmesan
200 g (7 oz/2 cups) dry breadcrumbs
Cinnamon and nutmeg, to taste

It's almost compulsory for Italians to serve *cappelletti* during winter. These are also called *agnolini* but you must change the shape to a half-moon.

Cappelletti di Parma

To make filling Place oil and butter in a large heavy-based saucepan, add onion and cook over low heat for 5 minutes or until soft. Add celery and most of its leaves and cook for 3 minutes, then add carrot and cook for another 3 minutes. Increase heat to high and add meat, turning to brown on all sides. Add wine and cook until evaporated and the smell of alcohol has gone. Add tomato paste and enough brodo to cover the meat, reduce heat to low and simmer for 2–3 hours or until meat is tender. You may need to add some more brodo if looking a bit dry. Remove meat from sauce (reserving sauce for another dish) and, when cool, coarsely chop meat. Transfer to a bowl, add eggs, parmesan, breadcrumbs, cinnamon and nutmeg, season to taste and combine well. If the mixture is a little wet, add a bit more parmesan or breadcrumbs.

   To make cappelletti Follow instructions on page 54 for making pasta fresca, using the weights above. Cut sheets into 4 cm (1½ in) squares. Working with a few squares at a time and leaving remainder covered, place 1 teaspoon filling onto each square, then fold in half diagonally to form a triangle, bring corners together and pinch to seal. Place on a lightly floured tray in front of a fan to dry.

   Place remaining brodo in a saucepan. Remove all vegetables and chop half of them into julienne and return to the brodo with the remaining celery leaves (discard remaining vegetables). Bring brodo to the boil, add cappelletti and cook until al dente. Serve as you would serve a soup and with plenty of parmesan.

Serves 6

150 ml (5 fl oz) extra virgin
olive oil
1 garlic clove, finely chopped
2 tablespoons finely chopped
flat-leaf parsley
300 g (10½ oz) prosciutto,
finely chopped
150 g (5½ oz) pork sausages,
skins removed and crumbled

15 g (½ oz) porcini mushrooms,
soaked in warm water for
30 minutes, drained
and finely chopped
250 g (9 oz) fresh mixed mushrooms,
trimmed and chopped
A pinch of dried chilli flakes
500 ml (17 fl oz) vellutata (p225)
500 g (1 lb 2 oz) dried strozzapreti
Grated parmesan, to serve

This variety of pasta is from Romagna and is also known as *strangozzi* or *stringozzi*, their names mean 'priest chokers' or 'stranglers'. For the *vellutata*, double the recipe on page 225 and omit the garlic and walnuts.

Strozzapreti con Salsiccia e Prosciutto

STROZZAPRETI WITH SAUSAGE AND PROSCIUTTO

Place oil and garlic in a frying pan and cook over medium heat for 1 minute or until garlic is soft. Add parsley, prosciutto and sausage meat and cook, stirring, for 5–6 minutes or until meat is lightly browned. Add all the mushrooms and chilli flakes and simmer for about 15 minutes or until most of the water from the mushrooms has evaporated. Stir in *vellutata* and simmer for 3–5 minutes or until sauce is well combined and creamy.

Cook strozzapreti in salted boiling water until al dente. Drain and place in a serving bowl. Pour over sauce, toss until well combined and serve immediately with parmesan.

Serves 6

Light of Lucia La suocera Mother-in-law

4 litres (140 fl oz) meat or
vegetable brodo (see p84)
4 large eggs
Freshly grated nutmeg
6 tablespoons dry fine
breadcrumbs
2 tablespoons finely grated
parmesan, plus extra, to serve
2 tablespoons plain
(all-purpose) flour

This dish brings you back to your home, to your mother's arms. In Italy, the instrument used to make *passatelli* is similar to a potato ricer but has larger holes.

Passatelli

Bring the brodo to the boil in a large saucepan.

In a large bowl, beat the eggs, then add the nutmeg and season liberally. Gradually add the breadcrumbs, parmesan and flour to form a dough. Taste and check if more seasoning is needed. Place the dough in a potato ricer held over the brodo. Press the dough through the holes, using a knife to cut the passatelli to about 4 cm (1½ in) lengths and letting them fall into the stock. Once you have used all the dough, reduce the heat to low and simmer for 4 minutes. Serve the passatelli like you would serve soup with plenty of parmesan.

Serves 6

650 g (1 lb 7 oz) type '00' flour
(see glossary), plus extra for dusting
7g (⅛ oz) fresh yeast

This delicious bread takes three days to make but is well worth the wait. Made with just flour and water and no salt, it is the perfect companion to the often heavily seasoned food of Tuscany.

TUSCAN BREAD

Day 1 Place 300 g (10½ oz) of flour in a bowl. Make a well in the centre and pour in 180 ml (6 fl oz/¾ cup) of water. Crumble 5 g (⅛ oz) of yeast over the top. Stir water and yeast until well combined, then incorporate the flour until just combined. Stir as little as possible as you don't want to wake up the gluten. Cover bowl with a plate and stand for 24 hours.

Day 2 Transfer rested dough to a larger bowl. Add 50 ml (1½ fl oz) of water. Break the dough up with your hands and add 100 g (3½ oz) flour and form into a new dough. Do not work the dough, let it rest for another 24 hours.

Day 3 Place remaining 250 g (9 oz) flour in a large bowl, make a well in the centre, add 150 ml (5 fl oz) of water and remaining yeast. Stir water and yeast until well combined, then add rested dough, in pieces, and incorporate with the yeast mixture until well combined. Slowly add the flour, working as little as possible. Shape the dough into a log and place, smooth side up, on a flour-dusted, baking paper-lined oven tray. Dust dough liberally with flour and place a packet of flour or something similar underneath baking paper on either side of the dough to help retain its shape. Rest in a warm place for 1½ hours. Meanwhile, heat a pizza stone or heavy-based oven tray in a 220°C (425°F/Gas 7) oven. Carefully place dough on hot stone or tray and bake for 10 minutes. Reduce temperature to 180°C (350°F/Gas 4) and bake for 40 minutes or until base sounds hollow when tapped.

Makes 1 loaf

1 egg, lightly beaten
2 tablespoons pine nuts
Icing (confectioners') sugar,
for dusting

Pasta frolla
250 g (9 oz) plain (all-purpose) flour
120 g (4¼ oz) caster (superfine) sugar
120 g (4¼ oz) unsalted butter,
chilled, chopped
1 egg, plus 1 egg yolk

1½ teaspoons baking powder
Zest of 1 lemon

Crema pasticcera
2 eggs, plus 1 yolk
100 g (3½ oz) caster (superfine) sugar
50 g (1¾ oz) plain (all-purpose) flour
30 g (1 oz) unsalted butter,
softened
250 ml (9 fl oz/1 cup) milk
250 ml (9 fl oz/1 cup) cream

This is a classical Tuscan cake. You may find a variation with chocolate custard called *torta del nonno*.

Torta della Nonna

CUSTARD AND PINE NUT TART

To make pasta frolla Place flour, sugar and a pinch of salt in a food processor, add the butter and using the pulse action, process until mixture resembles fine breadcrumbs. Add the egg and yolk, baking powder and lemon zest and pulse just until pastry comes together. Be careful not to overwork the pastry. Remember the rule of *pasta frolla*: the uglier, the better! Shape into a ball, wrap in plastic wrap and refrigerate for 30 minutes.

To make crema pasticcera Whisk the eggs, yolk, sugar, flour, butter and a pinch of salt until smooth. Place milk and cream in a saucepan, bring to the boil. While whisking continuously, gradually add to the egg mixture and combine well. Return mixture to the pan and cook over low heat, whisking continuously, for 5 minutes or until thick and smooth. Remove from heat and cool.

Preheat oven to 180°C (350°F/Gas 4). Roll out two-thirds of the pastry on a lightly floured surface until 5 mm (¼ in) thick and use to line base and side of a 23 cm (9 in) tart tin with removable base. Pour over cooled custard. Roll out remaining pastry, place on top of custard, pressing edge gently to seal and trim excess pastry. Brush with beaten egg, sprinkle with pine nuts and bake for 30–40 minutes or until golden. Serve warm or at room temperature, dusted with icing sugar.

Serves 8

Pasta technique

Kneading dough

Gluten is necessary to give the dough elasticity and kneading increases the rate of gluten formation. If the flour was simply mixed with eggs and made into a dough, the formation of gluten would occur too slowly.

Resting dough

The gluten in dough needs to rest and absorb water. After 30 minutes of resting, the starch grains in the dough will have absorbed moisture from the atmosphere which breaks down the starch allowing the protein in the gluten to soften and become more pliable and elastic. This in turn helps the dough stay intact when passing through the pasta machine.

Pasta machine settings

If you have followed my recipes and kneaded the dough for about 6–10 minutes, there is no need to pass the dough through the Number 1 setting again and again. In fact, if you do this, you will be at risk of over-kneading your dough, making the pasta too soft.

Storing dough

If you do not have the time to continue preparing your pasta, you can place the dough in a covered bowl or airtight container in the fridge and carry on over the next day or two. The dough will darken in colour as it has no preservatives. The colour will return to normal once it has been passed through the pasta machine. It may have absorbed a little moisture and become too sticky, though, so add a little flour. As for the freezer? Pasta dough cannot be frozen.

Freezing pasta

Freeze fresh pasta in a single layer on a floured tray and, once frozen, you can keep it in a plastic bag in the freezer for up to 3 months.

Storing fresh pasta

Before refrigerating fresh pasta, ensure it has been fully dried by the fan so it doesn't stick to the tea towel (dish towel). (Forget about fighting with the tea towel; it will always win.) If you do have trouble removing the pasta from the tea towel, simply place the tea towel with the pasta attached into boiling, salted water and after a few minutes, remove the tea towel. The pasta will loosen without tearing apart.

Drying pasta

Drying pasta properly before cooking makes it sturdier and and better able to hold its shape during cooking. This is especially true for filled pastas such as ravioli, which are very moist and need to be totally dry before cooking in order to withstand the boiling water. Use a fan to speed up the drying process.

When making long pasta such as tagliatelle, if you do not dry the fresh pasta sheets before cutting, the strands will stick together immediately. On the other hand, if you over-dry pasta sheets, they will become brittle. So make sure the pasta sheets are dried but pliable before you put them through a pasta machine.

Sealing filled pasta

If you are having trouble sealing filled pasta such as ravioli, brush the pasta with beaten egg. Do not, under any circumstances, spray or sprinkle water on the pasta.

Glossary

'0' flour
The best flour to make fresh egg pasta as it carries the *ceneri*, a mineral which makes the pasta more rustic in texture and has a precious aroma. Available from select Italian delicatessens and gourmet food stores.

'00' flour
Widely available outside Italy and a good substitute for '0' flour when making fresh egg pasta. This is also an excellent flour for making cakes as it is the finest.

Alchermes
A red-coloured liqueur made from flowers and spices. Available from select bottle stores.

Castelluccio lentils
Famous for their delicate taste and tiny size – only 2 mm (1/16 in) in diameter. They are found on the Castelluccio plain of Umbria, below the legendary Sibillini Mountains. Since 1998 the lentil produced in Castelluccio di Norcia has been awarded the IGT, or Protected Geographical Indication.

Cavolo nero
Literally meaning black cabbage, this Tuscan cabbage is widely used and available.

Cedro
Also known as citron, this Sicilian fruit is used for eating, not juicing and are often preserved and candied.

Cotechino or cotechino di Modena
A sausage made from pork and its rind, and, as its name suggests, comes from Modena. Cotechino is often served with lentils or cannellini beans in a sauce alongside polenta, especially around the New Year.

Garganelli tray
Traditional trays used in Romagna to make their famous garganelli. If you are in Australia you can order them from www.cucinaitaliana.com.au or use a clean comb and chopstick.

Giardiniera
Also called *sotto aceti*, this refers to vegetables such as onions, celery, zucchini, carrots and cauliflower which are pickled in red or white wine vinegar.

Grano cotto per la pastiera
Cooked wheat sold in jars ready to use. Widely available in local Italian delicatessens. During Easter in Italy, people used to buy the grains cooked in the traditional way from their local bakery to eat during their Easter feast.

Guanciale
Its name is derived from *guancia*, Italian for cheek. The cheeks are cured for 3 weeks in salt, pepper and sometimes chilli. The flavour is stronger than pancetta and the texture more delicate. It is a delicacy of the regions of Umbria and Lazio.

Mandolino
This is not a mandolin to cut vegetables. It is a traditional bamboo scoop used in the Emilia Romagna region to remove the tagliatelle from the pan. It is the best way to remove fresh pasta as it will not damage the pasta, while also retaining some of its moisture, which is eliminated when drained in colanders. The name comes from the musical instrument.

Maraschino
A liqueur made with marasca cherries, featuring the cherry's distinctive flavour.

Pancetta

Pork belly that has been salt-cured and spiced.

Ricotta salata

A sheep's milk cheese, pure white in colour with a dense but slightly spongy texture and a salty, milky flavour like a dry feta.

Salted capers

Capers are the buds of a flowering shrub. The shrub produces capers of various sizes, the smallest are the most valued.

The best salted capers come from Pantelleria, a tiny, volcanic island off the coast of Sicily. To retain their flavour and texture they are placed in a jar with sea salt.

The brine version is not as good as the salted variety as the capers lose some of their flavour and texture in the brine.

Before using salted capers, soak in water for 15 minutes. Rinse, then soak again for another 15 minutes or until ready to use.

Tuma

A sheep's milk cheese from Sicily. It's called *tuma* when eaten right out of the mould, *primo sale* when slightly salted, and *vastedda* when it has aged.

Wild fennel

Once you recognise this beautiful herb you'll notice that it grows wild all around you. It grows to about two metres high (about 6 feet), and has long, thin stems, yellow flowers and aniseed-flavoured feathery leaves. You can substitute with the stems of traditional fennel however the flavour is not as intense.

Index

Thank you

Thank you God, wherever you are, in blue days, in blue skies, in rays of sunshine… thank you Lord for inspiring me and letting me teach with full love and enthusiasm.

To my guardian angel, I thank him, too. You have always shone light on my path and never let me stay too long in the dark.

Thank you Natasha Milner who upon attending one of my classes encouraged me to write this book. Natasha managed to photograph my soul, wrapped it and hand gifted it to Jane Lawson from Murdoch Books. Furthermore the outstanding photography of this book is thanks to the touch of art of Natasha.

Thank you to Jane Lawson who understood immediately what the book was all about and held the Italian flag high helping us to save this cause, to save Italian food and traditions.

And the whole team at Murdoch Books, I thank them for their talent, for their love and understanding and their professionalism. I was gifted with a team who could understand Italy and their spirit. From Carla Grossetti to my editor Daniela Bertollo, who was in charge of all aspects of editing this book. Daniela identified herself with so many stories of the book that sometimes I could see Lucia printed there in the colour of her eyes!

The designer was simply outstanding. Behind the scenes, a beautiful girl called Emilia Toia. Her eye for detail and imagination have given Lucia the light you see in this book. Sarah O'Brien took care of the food styling. She was in charge of the eye which will feed the camera, that will tempt you to go home and make all these recipes.

Thank you to my assistants: Ai Nagoya and Yuka Kishimoto – simply the best, simply irreplaceable.

Thank you to my everyday heroes, my three musketeers: Andrew, Luca and Antonella. Their love has guided me to deliver these words, words of passion, words of hope, words that inspired me to continue my work: to save my country's culture. They have always believed in me. I would have never made it without their support.

I have also been fortunate to have been adopted into my new family on this side of the world. I thank my in-laws – they welcomed me into their family, the Russell family, sweetly known by us as the Geebs.

As I lost my Dad while in the process of writing this book, I have run to the arms of my wonderful friend, a father to me, Renzo Franceschini. Together we have won many battles in the name of our country. We are here to serve, we are here to love Italy, indefinitely no matter what. Thank you, Renzo, for being an inspiration, for being determined to define the Italian flavours.

Last, but not least, thank you to the Simili sisters – your work will never be forgotten as generations will go by learning the correct flavours, learning the essence of real Italian cooking.

Published in 2010 by Murdoch Books Pty Limited

Murdoch Books Australia
Pier 8/9
23 Hickson Road
Millers Point NSW 2000
Phone: +61 (0) 2 8220 2000
Fax: +61 (0) 2 8220 2558
www.murdochbooks.com.au

Murdoch Books UK Limited
Erico House, 6th Floor
93–99 Upper Richmond Road
Putney, London SW15 2TG
Phone: +44 (0) 20 8785 5995
Fax: +44 (0) 20 8785 5985
www.murdochbooks.co.uk

Publisher: Jane Lawson
Project Editor: Daniela Bertollo
Designer: Emilia Toia
Food Photographer: Natasha Milne
Additional photography: Jane Burton Taylor, Co.As.It, Julie Renouf, Natasha Milne
Stylist: Sarah O'Brien
Editors: Micaela di Piramo & Carla Grossetti
Food Editor: Christine Osmond
Production: Alexandra Gonzalez

National Library of Australia Cataloguing-in-Publication Data

Author: Luciana Sampogna
Title: Light of Lucia: A celebration of Italian life, love and food
ISBN: 9781741965087 (hbk.)
Notes: Includes index.
Subjects: Cookery, Italian
                 Italy – Social life and customs.
Dewey Number: 641.5945

A catalogue record for this book is available from the British Library.

PRINTED IN CHINA

IMPORTANT: Those who might be at risk from the effects of salmonella poisoning (the elderly, pregnant women, young children and those suffering from immune deficiency diseases) should consult their doctor with any concerns about eating raw eggs.

OVEN GUIDE: You may find cooking times vary depending on the oven you are using. For fan-forced ovens, as a general rule, set the oven temperature to 20°C (35°F) lower than indicated in the recipe.